Praise for *Don't Wear Shoes You Can't Walk In*

"…a jaunty guide that has plenty of personality. Wise, witty, and worthwhile advice for readers navigating their twenties."

—*Kirkus Reviews*

"Brilliantly articulated, perfectly digestible. *Don't Wear Shoes You Can't Walk In* should be required reading for when anyone turns twenty."

—GenTwenty

"A manual for navigating new beginnings, no matter your age. Timeless advice paired with relatable learnings to help you uncover your next best step forward."

—Natalie Franke, cofounder of The Rising Tide Society and author of *Built to Belong*

"An insightful book from a talented, introspective and passionate writer. I found myself relating to so much of Michelle's self-exploration, and I know this will be an impactful read for many others.

—Stacy Stahl, founder of How They Asked and Sweeter Cards

"An empowering, practical, hands-on guide that will help the twentysomethings in your life create more meaningful, manageable lives."

—Kristen Hadeed, Leadership Thought Leader and author of *ɹ Up*

T0061871

"The handbook I wish I'd had throughout my twenties, filled with compassionate guidance from a time-tested big sister who wants you to learn from her experience but also forge your own path every step of the way. Michelle Douglas has an uncanny ability to take life's deep, nuanced lessons and package them into clever metaphors that will stick with you long after you put this book down."

—Caroline Kelso Zook, author of
Your Brightest Life Journal

"A joyous guidebook . . . the writing prompts will be helpful to anyone of any age."

—Jo Giese, award-winning radio journalist and
author of *Never Sit If You Can Dance*

"These are lessons we all need to know to succeed in life but are not taught in school. This book will inspire you to achieve your dreams."

—Whitney Holtzman, CEO of Social Victories, NFL
Agent, and author of *You Are the First You*

"Douglas offers both practical and sage advice on everything from starting careers, cultivating relationships, and creating an overall balanced life. *Don't Wear Shoes You Can't Walk In* is a wonderful and useful book for a young person starting out on their own."

—Kristen Rademacher, M.Ed. Academic Coach,
University of North Carolina at Chapel Hill

DON'T WEAR SHOES YOU CAN'T WALK IN

DON'T WEAR SHOES YOU CAN'T WALK IN

A Field Guide for Your Twenties

Michelle Douglas

Published 2022
Printed in the United States of America
Print ISBN: 978-1-64742-320-9
E-ISBN: 978-1-64742-321-6

Library of Congress Control Number: 2021918921

For information, address:
She Writes Press
1569 Solano Ave #546
Berkeley, CA 94707

She Writes Press is a division of SparkPoint Studio, LLC.

To Adelaide—

This was written for you, even before I knew you.

Keep taking big steps.

CONTENTS

INTRODUCTION

Life in your early twenties can be confusing and uncertain. It's an exciting time that can also feel chaotic, filled with new adventures, relationships, and emotions. The next ten years are formidable years and, in this time, you will find yourself encountering new situations and thinking some of these thoughts: Can I survive in a city where I only know one person? How do I find purpose outside of work? Is it okay to date more than one person in the same week? Am I successful? How do I even define success?

It's time to ensure that the years to come are everything you want them to be. Free of confusion and chaos, rich in meaningful relationships, satisfying to the soul, and full of opportunity for joy and growth. But how will you find your way? Imagine if you had advice from someone who has experienced what you are about to go through—moving, working, loving, losing, quitting, building, and all the while maintaining a strong sense of self.

If you are a recent college graduate, new city transplant, career shifter, or anyone on the journey that is being a twentysomething, you've opened the right book. The pages that follow offer relatable advice in the areas of work, love, practical adult life, and personal growth. Going beyond advice alone, this book provides the opportunity to explore yourself with prompts at the end of each chapter for you to answer, revealing the insights and wisdom you've already gained but might not realize you possess. Ultimately, this book aims to disrupt the routines of your daily life with a new filter placed on interactions and activities, one that will inspire you to ask on a regular basis, "Why is this moment happening in my life and what can I learn from it?"

In 2010, when I graduated from college and moved to a new city for work, I found myself asking the same questions. I knew this would be not only a time I'd want to remember, but also one where I wished I had a guide. So I wanted to create one for my future children. I committed to the practice of writing down one thing I learned every day that year. Since then, I've recorded my thoughts, my days, and the important lessons that life taught and brought me as I began to fully explore my life and learn its strengths, weaknesses, and most importantly, its cycles. These lessons now exist in six volumes of black leather Moleskine journals, and I consider them to be among my most prized possessions and one of the greatest things I've ever done for myself. Whether you decide to make it a journal, a note on your phone, or a running document on your computer, I encourage you to take inventory of your own life. Reflecting on each day as it happens and learning from it changes the way you view and approach the next day and every day after that.

My hope is that this book allows you to learn from my

life, but even more so, teaches you how to enhance your own life by being aware of and open to the lessons happening all around you and acknowledging what they can teach you.

Recognize them. Record them. And you will grow because of them.

TITLE LESSON

Don't wear shoes you can't walk in.

Over the past ten years, "Don't wear shoes you can't walk in" is a lesson that has revealed itself to me many times. I first learned it when I borrowed a pair of high heels from a friend for a job interview. The shoes were not only too high for me, but I began to get blisters before I even made it into the building where I was to be interviewed. As I stumbled and shuffled across the threshold into the hiring manager's office, I couldn't help but worry that my clear physical discomfort translated to a visible lack of confidence. I didn't get that job, and sometimes I wondered if it was because I didn't put my best foot forward. After all, I could barely put one foot in front of the other. The way we walk says a lot about us—not just our physical presence, but our state of mind. The takeaway here is simple: You should never wear shoes you can't walk in.

Of course, this lesson speaks to more than just literal shoes. It's also about being true to yourself and not trying to be someone you are not. If you are wearing shoes you can't walk in, and thus denying your authentic self, you likely won't make it where you're trying to go.

It's a lesson that sums up so much of the decade that is your twenties. Sometimes people, jobs, and activities won't fit into your life, but you'll wish they did. Sometimes other options will look better than what you currently have, but once you obtain them, you realize they aren't more desirable at all. Over time, you'll learn that reliability is more valuable than glamour and that knowing yourself is the best way to get where you're going. Recognizing and recording the lessons of your life can change your path for the better.

1 PERSONAL GROWTH

You're not here because you're like everyone else; you're here because you're you.

Upon graduation from college, I moved to Atlanta, Georgia to begin my dream of working in advertising. About a year and a half after I moved to Atlanta, my older brother also moved there for work. I was working in account management at the Atlanta arm of a New York advertising agency, and he was a graphic designer for one of the most well-known design firms in the southeast. By some of the goals we'd set for ourselves earlier in life, we'd made it! We lived less than ten minutes away from each other, and being adults together in the same city felt like a gift, as we'd had a close relationship even when we lived far away.

Every Friday, my brother was responsible for contributing a blog post to his company's website, which meant that every Thursday evening, either in person or by phone, I was reading and editing his draft. I enjoyed the role of being his sounding board and editor, an additional weeknight obligation that I happily took on. Maybe I should have added "Editor or Guest Contributor" to my own résumé after this season of life.

One Thursday night over the phone, we found ourselves discussing our skills and our roles within our teams at work. He was still very new to his team, and he was asking the questions that we all ask in some form when we're encountering new experiences and new relationships: Where do I fit in with this group of incredibly talented people? How can I best contribute? What is my role here?

I wasn't new at my job anymore; I had been there for over a year at that point, but his questions still resonated with me. No matter how comfortable or well acquainted we become, these questions remain relevant as we constantly evaluate and reconsider our days, striving to live our most effective and fulfilling lives. Our late-night blog editing conversation brought my brother to an unforgettable line, one that he said aloud more to himself than to me, "You're not here because you're like everyone else; you're here because you're you."

It was an idea he landed on suddenly, that he didn't need to be just like his coworkers, they each had their own role. To him it was a reminder of his purpose, his contribution, why he had been hired. He had been hired not because he fit a pre-existing shape, but because his individual talents and qualities made his company and his team more whole than they were before. He said this line and wrote it down that night for himself, and it was published on the blog the next day amidst other tips for taking on new challenges and playing one's role on a team. But I wrote it down because I needed to hear it and remember it too.

I've always been very self-assured and disciplined in working to improve, but I've also always been eager to earn praise and garner reputation. In the early years of adulthood, it can be too easy to prioritize success and achievement and lose sight of who you are. You may quickly, and without even realizing it, find yourself working toward becoming someone you read about in a magazine or saw on LinkedIn. During this time in my life, I wasn't always keenly aware of how I moved my marker for success based on the achievements and actions of others. I needed to remind myself that I wasn't here to be just like my roommate or coworker, that I didn't need to strive for the exact same things that my college friends were accomplishing. I was here, in this job, in this relationship, in this community, to be uniquely me and to strengthen my surroundings in ways that only I could.

How you define yourself, and the lens through which you view yourself, will shape many of the interactions and experiences that lie ahead. Personal growth can be something of a Trojan horse; it doesn't always come in the ways you expect it to. Sure, it comes in the shape of learning to listen actively from a heart-to-heart with a best friend, or learning to remain measured in your confidence after an exceptionally poor or positive performance review. But it also comes from unmemorable decisions you made, simple acts you repeat every day, and events that don't even happen to you at all. And most of the time, you see or feel the result of that growth only after the fact.

Personal growth can also be the realization of your own limitations, learning how to give yourself a quick fix of confidence, and finding the strength to keep going. Remember, you're not here because you're like everyone else; you're here because you're you. For once, it's truly all about you and recognizing the opportunities that exist to enhance the incredible being that you already are. This chapter delivers lessons in all of the topics that start with "self-" . . . think confidence, awareness, doubt, motivation, and discipline. They are all necessary tools that will help you on your path. Like me, you'll learn that it's okay if that path doesn't unfold as you imagine it will. In fact, I hope it doesn't. Because you'll grow much more from the missteps and mistakes than you will if you get it "right" right away.

1 The greatest mountain ranges have more than one peak.

Your career and life are like those great mountain ranges. They don't peak just once. Five years into my working career, I found myself in a job that by many other people's standards would have been stellar. Great office setup and company culture, fairly predictable and standard nine-to-five hours, regular team-building events and staff workouts. The problem was I'd done a similar job before and I knew how to do it well. Nothing about my work was really new or challenging to me. I was often tormented by the clock, trying to make it to the end of the day. I longed to be in a different role at a different company.

The longing to be somewhere else made the lack of vigor at the job even harder. I often drove home at night wondering if this unchallenging and predictable nine-to-five was all I was capable of anymore, asking myself, "Is this it? Has my career already peaked?" Thankfully, my internal voice had learned to be a good coach over the years. When I asked myself if I'd peaked, the image of a mountain range came to mind and I realized that those ranges have many peaks. I was simply on my way to the next one. If you were once talented and impressive, you still are. Talent doesn't just go away. When you are in a valley, remind yourself that there are more peaks, work hard for them, and be ready to enjoy them when you get there.

2   As you grow, adjust your fairy tale.

At the age of twenty-one, my fairy tale sounded something like this: move to a big city, live within walking distance of work, and move up in my advertising career as fast as possible. I envisioned moving every few years, to other big cities, collecting as much professional and geographic experience as I could. At age twenty-six, after living in only one big city, I moved to Annapolis, Maryland, a place I didn't know anything about and that I can promise you was never on my map or in my plan. I moved for another person, also something I never thought I'd do. I was thrilled to meet a life partner in the first city I stopped in—that part alone is its own fairy tale—but that also drastically changed the rest of my dream.

With the unplanned change in location, I unexpectedly found myself in a smaller town, living in a house with a driveway instead of a walk-up, and, rather than being within walking distance of my office, I was a very long commute from the city where I worked at a job I didn't love. None of this was quite what I had envisioned for myself. But the change in location prompted me to achieve other dreams I'd started to recognize, like working for a large athletic brand and even starting my own business. I learned that as we grow, we must adjust the fairy tale we've written for ourselves. If you change an important part of your circumstance, like choosing a life partner, having a baby, or going back to school and redirecting your career, then you also have to consider the changes in outcome that might come as a result of those decisions. Letting go of your dream doesn't mean that life isn't still a dream, it's just a different one.

3   Kick the nearest shark.

In other words, do what you need to survive, first. I'm sure you have a lot going on in your world. Things like new jobs, new cities, new apartments and bills, maintaining new and old relationships, taking on new associations and obligations, these things can all make you feel like you are drowning at times. Figure out what is your nearest shark, the issue or commitment that's closest to pulling you under. Instead of trying to take on multiple things at once, just tackle that one important thing first.

4   You will learn the roads.

New is exciting, but it can also be filled with uncertainty. It takes time, but soon enough you'll be familiar with a landscape that was previously unknown. When I learned this lesson, I had just moved into a new home and was out for a run. I believe we can do our best exploring on foot. But while I was out seeking new discoveries, I got lost and realized I needed to learn the roads. This was before everyone ran with their phones, and I've never liked doing that anyway. As I slowed to a walk and eventually found my way home, I reminded myself that I'd soon find my fastest and favorite routes, that it just takes time.

This concept has proved true for my work life too. Situations like navigating relationships with a new boss or finding the best way to your desk from the campus parking lot can be uncharted territory at first. But you'll learn their ways of working and you'll find the best path for you. In time, you'll have mastered all that was once unknown, shaving minutes off your morning routine and finding comfort in familiarity. Not only will you learn the roads, but then you'll make room in your brain and in your life to take on more unknowns.

5 Don't just take what is given to you.

If you want more, ask for it, work for it, and exhaust your resources to find what it is you were hoping for.

6 Everything you put into the world is something people could talk about. Make sure everything you say and do are things you wouldn't mind reading about later.

You may have had a parent who told you not to send pictures of yourself to anyone on the internet. That's very good advice; listen to them. This lesson may sound similar, but it isn't just a reminder not to send inappropriate photos to anyone in your contact list. It's also a reminder to be thoughtful about everything you send, text, tweet, snap, post, write, etc. Words and images are equally dangerous.

Early in my career, I had coworkers who would send personal correspondence over work email, and it made me uncomfortable. I often wanted to respond and be friendly or participate in the banter, but I was always very nervous about the content being shared, too. There was talk of other coworkers, personal accounts of nights out, and even a request or two for a date. I always felt as if, no matter what I typed in reply, there was risk involved. I was new and still navigating relationships, and it was important to me to maintain a professional reputation. There is an art to graciously declining interest while attempting to remain friends, all while being professional. Thankfully, I learned the important lesson of taking care about what you write early on in my career. A great litmus test is to review what you're writing and imagine it being read aloud at a staff meeting or retweeted by a media outlet. Everything we put out into the world can now be relayed through a megaphone, so make sure you'll be pleased, not embarrassed, to hear or read your words again.

7 Be so happy you lose yourself, but not your wallet.

I believe you can "let go" and "be responsible" at the same time. One of my best friends came to visit me in Atlanta from Florida. At the time she was a law student, presumably smart and responsible, which is correct. We spent much of the day on Saturday frolicking around town. We lay in Piedmont Park, reading magazines and drinking wine; we buzzed and skipped along idyllic streets with cute shops, stopping for an afternoon ice cream, and shopping here and there. I specifically remember that my friend made a purchase at some point in the day because she was carrying, actually more like blissfully swinging, a small brown gift bag as we skipped our way back to my house. When we got home and were later preparing for an evening out, she discovered she had lost her credit card and driver's license.

We retraced our steps, this time with significantly less skipping and buzzing, but unfortunately, we came up empty. It tarnished our glowing image of the afternoon we'd just had and made things like having an ID for her plane ride home more complicated. It's highly encouraged to be so happy and feel so light that you want to skip your way home. I hope your twenties are filled with many moments that make you throw your arms up in the air. But before you do that, just pause quickly to make sure your wallet isn't in your hand. You'll be even happier later when you've lost yourself, but not your stuff.

8   Defining moments are often the ones when we choose to say "no."

We're conditioned to believe that the biggest moments in our lives come when we say "yes." Yes to a job offer or a marriage proposal, or finally saying yes to a new home after a long journey to find it. All of the times we say yes are big and important, but many of the times we say no are equally defining for our lives. I've said no to a request for a date, and that no kept me available for the next person who asked. I've said no to a job offer from a former client, and that no reminded me that I had done my job in the best way possible because my client wanted to take me with them—but I stayed and got a promotion instead. I've said no to an offer to move to a different city, and that no kept me in a city I loved longer to grow a more meaningful relationship with a now lifelong mentor. I've said no to another job offer from a dream company, and that no freed me up to start my own business.

Pay close attention the next time you say no to something; it's possible that it can equally be defined as a big yes to something else. Life really is like a choose-your-own-ending book; each time you say yes or no, you are directing your path.

9   Try things three times (foods, activities, exercises).

First, to get over the fear of doing it. Second, to learn how to do it properly. Third, to decide if you enjoy doing it now that you know what you're doing.

10   Speak up, even if you are the seemingly least important or smallest person in the room.

Have you ever earned a seat at the table, but immediately been afraid of losing it? When I was twenty-eight, I started working for one of the world's largest apparel and footwear brands, alongside some amazing veterans in the industry. I had a background in sports and my own expertise; I had earned my spot there, but sometimes I found myself feeling small as I gratefully sat among giants. I was eager to learn from them and also eager to earn their trust and praise. At times this led me to think I should keep my head down and my pen out, diligently taking notes. At other times it led me to look out and confidently share my point of view. I learned that you are in the room and at the table because you have something to offer, and hopefully it's not just your note-taking skills. Don't waste your spot or someone else's. Step up, speak up, and offer what you think and know.

11 Don't dwell on the past. Focus on what you can do now, not what you should have done then.

12 Out on the trail, you will doubt yourself, but don't let it change your course.

Self-doubt and negative self-talk are brutal. They can dampen your spirit and your potential. They can paralyze you and, most tragically, they can redirect the course of your life. Whether the trail is entrepreneurship, a physical walking path, or studying for an important postgraduate standardized test, know that you will have self-doubt. You will question yourself and the decisions you've made. Be prepared for self-doubt, and push through it; don't let it alter the path you've chosen.

13   Sometimes we all have to appear to be brave even when we are not.

14   Focus on the things you want to be good at. Don't get distracted by things others are good at.

In my early twenties, I often moved my own marker for success based on the actions of others. I touched on this topic briefly in the introduction to this chapter. But it's only in hindsight that I recognize this and can admit it. When I was in the moment, caught up in the idea that motion equaled progress, I didn't realize that I was constantly moving the finish line, not necessarily moving toward it. Coming out of college, I had a lot of really successful friends who got great jobs in big cities, were published for starting new ventures, and made it onto "30 Under 30" lists. Based on the achievements of others, I would rethink some of my own plans and say to myself, "Maybe I should consider a role in digital or tech," "Maybe I should go to business school," or "Maybe I should start making a product on the side."

But I wasn't good at digital, standardized tests, or making products. I was really good at building and cultivating relationships with creatives and clients. I was developing a passion for social impact without knowing it yet, and I loved the work and world of branding. If your friend publishes a book, be excited for her, but don't think you have to start writing one yourself. If your old coworkers land jobs at Google, Apple, and Amazon, don't be upset with the decision you made to go work for nonprofits. Clearly you had a different end goal in mind. Let the success of others motivate you, pushing you toward your own goals, not toward theirs.

15   Remember that it's likely you'll create something similar everywhere you go, so when you are seeking that newness and difference, remember your nature.

You might still be in your years of firsts: first job, first apartment, first new couch, first new relationship out of college. So you may not know this yet, but you have your own style and you are still curating your own taste. These things are all a development of you; they are choices, not coincidences. As time passes and you age with your firsts, you may become bored or antsy for something new again. There are some easy ways to accomplish a feeling of newness and freshness; you can get a haircut, buy a new couch, paint a wall, or quit your job and move to an entirely new city, but one thing won't change much, and that's you.

There's an old saying that comes to mind: "Wherever you go, there you are." It's true; even when I took myself out of the situations I was in, moved cities, changed jobs, or freshened up my surroundings in some way, I found that many of my emotions or the themes of my life didn't change. It was still me, slowly building a similar routine and community. Only so much of your life is created by external factors. Most of it is actually created by you, chosen by your preferences, your outlook, and your taste for life.

16   Make sure your voice consistently communicates what you believe in.

17   All of that happened so you could handle all of this.

"You are always right where you are supposed to be." It's a popular phrase that sometimes makes you feel good or sometimes doesn't, like when you're stranded on the side of the road with car trouble or you hate your job and can't secure a different one. But I do believe that God and the world are working for us and with us, and that we're always right where we're supposed to be. My car battery once died in a parking spot next to a car owned by a talented mechanic who was able to jump-start my car and remove the battery at the same time. I once rode in an Uber with a stranger who referred me to a future client. And I also just happened to start my own business writing brand messaging for nonprofits around the same time a professional athlete I had previously worked with was starting her own foundation—and she hired me. Wherever you are right now, on this couch, on this plane, next to this person, it's all for a reason.

Similarly, I believe the events that challenge us in life are conditioning us for something else that is in store. An illness in the family, an uncomfortable interaction with a boss, a job that you never thought you'd take, a breakup that left you in bed for days; each of these situations happened to prepare you for something else that is to come. It might not make sense yet, or you might never get to make sense of it. But your struggles really do help you grow and develop your strengths. Your trials are training you. Embrace them the very best you can.

18 We are all just works in progress.

Remember that of yourself and of others.

19 Be the kind of person who turns the light off when leaving a room.

It shows that you recognize the importance of preserving resources, and that you're considerate of others. No matter what your circumstances in life, whether you are successful and wealthy or just making it, don't forget this.

20 Always run through the finish.

Working in running events, I've had the opportunity to see many finish-line moments and the range of human emotions that happen there. Tears of joy, tears of pain, pride, victory, defeat. But there's never been a finish-line moment with a lesson as powerful as the one that became the photo finish of the 2015 Peachtree Road Race in Atlanta. The first male runner to approach the finish line threw his hand up in the air, celebrating what he thought was his victory, and in that very moment, he was passed by another runner. It was the closest finish in race history, the difference in time being nine one-hundredths of a second. It felt like something you might read or hear about (and it was indeed all over the national news that day), but to see it firsthand really drove this lesson home. Don't let up when you think the end is in sight, and don't celebrate your victories before they've happened. Whether it be a work project, an actual athletic race, a journey to better health, or even just a long drive home, see it through to the finish and then let yourself relax and relish your accomplishment.

21   Everyone must learn their own limitations.

My husband is a do-it-yourself kind of guy, and our home and wallets have benefitted greatly from this fine quality. He is a talented carpenter and builder, but not so handy when it comes to repairs involving water and plumbing. Those never tend to go his way. The importance of testing limits came to me after he flooded our basement for a third time. I was angrily wringing out towels but also grateful that he tries to do things himself. The only way to know you can't do it is to try.

22   Believe you are capable until proven otherwise.

23   Being your best self means finding that place of balance where you're present and fully participating in both your professional and personal lives.

As you age you'll hear more and more about balance. When I was a kid, balance was what you did on the beam or to get on your bicycle. But in my adult life I've learned that balance is more than a physical act, it's also a feeling. Balance is comfortable and happy and sometimes peaceful too. As a young twentysomething, it can be hard to achieve balance. It seems the pendulum swings too far to work or too far to fun, which is then perceived as a lack of focus. For me, I've always found balance or happiness in my personal life when I'm succeeding professionally. My professional contributions have an impact on the way I perceive myself, which in turn impacts the way I show up in my personal life. Once I identified this, I was able to adjust my amounts accordingly. It's helpful to visualize an old scale, the kind you stand on at a doctor's office, and slowly inch the sliding weights of personal and professional life back and forth until you find what works for you.

24   Champions don't need perfect conditions to perform their best.

I overheard something like this during the Kentucky Derby the year American Pharaoh won the Triple Crown. It was a terribly muddy and rainy course, and greatness was still achieved by a creature expected to be great. I've observed that being great in perfect conditions is easier than being great no matter the condition, but that rougher conditions are what prove the greatness. So it was a reminder to not wait for perfect conditions, but just to go ahead and work to be great.

25   Live in a bigger city at some point in your life.

Cities! Oh, just thinking about them excites my senses. I love the smells, sounds, and sights, and the fact that there's always someone to watch and something to enjoy. But what I love even more is how cities open your eyes to new ideas, people, and cultures. Moving to Atlanta right out of college did this for me. If you are from a small town or grew up in a suburb, I'd recommend that you live in a city that's larger than the one you grew up in at some point in your life. Even if only for a short time. It will not only open your eyes but maybe even your mind, and change your perspective on a thing or two.

26   Only stand for more of the same if the same is something good.

27 No voice is too small.

My dad spent the majority of my life asking the city to clean up an empty lot near our house. We lived in a small, quiet, and quaint neighborhood, but on the drive into the neighborhood there was a desolate, city-owned piece of property where people would often dump trash or place things for sale. This particularly bothered my dad—he'd always taught us to take good care of our things, and to him this included the drive into our neighborhood. When I was a kid, our family would frequently clean up that empty lot. My brother and I would hop in the back of our dad's truck with trash bags and gloves and call ourselves "The Litter Patrol." In addition to our boots-on-the-ground efforts as "The Litter Patrol," my dad would also write letters to our local representatives in attempts to beautify the space and give it purpose. Fifteen years later, when I was in my early twenties, my dad texted me a photo of the lot. The city had planted four rows of trees to make it look nicer and to deter others from littering. It's beautiful, and my dad's persistence in this effort is a constant reminder that a single voice can make a difference. No matter what you may think, no voice is too small.

Prompt: What are you using or would you like to use your voice to change?

_____

_____

_____

_____

28   You learn the most from the moments when you feel the most vulnerable.

"Most vulnerable" might not seem like it's going to be most valuable, but it can be, it's true. I've learned a great deal from moments when I felt vulnerable or out of my comfort zone because it meant there was a lot at stake for me. I felt it when I said yes to a long-distance relationship with the man who is now my husband, after months of saying I didn't want to be in one. And I felt it when I decided to leave my "dream job" and start my own business. These moments are often accompanied by a full sensorial experience: think sweaty, heart-racing, crumpling-your-pro/con-list kinds of moments. You'll know them when you feel them; don't be afraid of them, they are helping you grow.

Prompt: When was the last time you felt really vulnerable or challenged to get out of your comfort zone? What did you learn from it?

_____

_____

_____

_____

_____

29   Practice the art of noticing without judging.

My first office in downtown Atlanta connected to many other office buildings by way of covered pedestrian bridges. It was great for people-watching and for being able to get lunch without going outside. Each day that I made my way through the covered bridges, or "tunnels," as we called them, I crossed paths with hundreds of strangers. One day I passed someone I'd never met who had the brightest green eyes. I immediately thought to myself, *I wonder if that's her real eye color?* I noticed how easy it can be to judge someone while you are quickly passing by, and I wondered if I was capable of observing without judging. Have you ever tried to just notice something about someone and stop there? I could have thought, *Her eyes are really green*, or *Dark hair, green eyes, skirt, walking quickly,* instead of *I wonder if that's her real eye color?* or *That skirt probably cost more than it's worth.* To observe without judgment is to focus on the facts of what you observe rather than the interpretations. Challenge yourself to observe and notice, and stop yourself each time your brain starts to make a judgment.

Prompt: Try this. The next time you are in public or sitting next to someone (maybe right now), notice something about someone without judging. Write it down here.

_____

_____

_____

_____

_____

_____

_____

_____

_____

_____

_____

30   When something bigger than you is in front of you, don't get too close. If it collapses, you'll need room to get out.

I was watching a small child stand in front of a very large TV when I thought to myself, *he should move in case it falls.* And then it occurred to me: We should all take this advice. Be cautious in the face of big ideas, big changes, big risks, big egos, and so on. Give yourself space to maneuver. Consider: If this idea or company fails, have I given myself enough room to get out safely, or will its fall crush me?

Prompt: Is there anything looming in front of you right now? Have you given yourself the space you need to be resilient if faced with adversity?

_____

_____

_____

_____

_____

_____

_____

31 Rinse out your own paintbrush. It's both youthful and replenishing.

Having or finding a hobby is another hard task in your early twenties. Much of your effort is given to the areas of work, learning to live on your own, romance, and maintaining friendships. If you are anything like me you've possibly asked yourself, "What do I do for fun?" or "What will I say when they ask if I have any hobbies?"

One night I was so determined to have a hobby that I forced myself to paint a small canvas. I sat outside with a glass of wine and some music, and I painted. It was a fine exercise and a pretty good time, but truthfully, I found the act of cleaning up to be more therapeutic than the act of painting itself. The chore of cleaning dirty paintbrushes may not seem restorative and rejuvenating, but it can be, once you reframe it. It reminds me of being a kid, and I've discovered that rinsing out a paintbrush is symbolic of cleansing and giving yourself a fresh start.

Prompt: Is there a daily task you could reframe, transforming it from a burden to a gift? What is it and how?

_____

_____

_____

_____

32   Think bigger! Try to imagine things that don't exist.

Don't limit yourself to what you already know, what you've already experienced, or what you can envision. In a later chapter of this book, you'll come across a lesson with a quote from Henry Ford that states, "If I had asked customers what they wanted, they would have said faster horses." This quote implies that people can only ask for what they know or understand. Don't let that be true for the way you think of yourself. When you're thinking about your future, your career, and how you might spend the rest of the days of your life, think bigger than what you already know. I've done this for myself, creating a business and a role I never could have imagined as my job when I first started working. I've also thought of two inventions that I'd love to spend my days working on, one for kids and one for the kitchen, and I'd tell you about them, but I'm going to hold on to them in the hope that one day they'll become real. It can be a great exercise to allow yourself to imagine with wild abandon.

Prompt: Write down something you've thought of, that you've otherwise never seen, heard of, or experienced. Things like a new planet to live on, a service or website you wish existed, or a product you could use but have never seen.

_____

_____

_____

_____

_____

_____

_____

_____

33 If you make mistakes, and you will, at least show yourself you learned from them.

This is the time of your life to make mistakes. In fact, it's critical that you make them. I say this because it's one of the best ways to learn. Mistakes can influence your preferences and they allow you to be a resource to others. Dwelling on your mistakes is a waste of time, but using those mistakes to improve yourself is not. I'll admit I'm a dweller myself, sometimes for days as I await a reply to an email I've sent, and sometimes only for the duration of an outing during which I feel immediate regret for not dressing properly for the weather. Not dwelling is a skill I've worked on through-out adulthood. In fact, I'm still actively working on it—just ask my husband. So, as a recovering dweller, I'm perfectly positioned to give you this advice: Make lots of mistakes. Then, instead of lamenting over what you did, envision and prepare for what you want to do the next time.

I made a memorable mistake when I moved to Maryland. I was so focused on work and so desperate to have a job that I accepted one with a one-and-a-half-hour commute. I prioritized a job over getting to know my community and learning how I might best be able to contribute there. Three months later I quit that same job because my health and happiness were in danger, but I learned an important lesson: Don't cling to work. This would become a recur-ring theme in my life, and it was an important lesson to have learned early. On a much smaller scale, I now also always take the time to thoughtfully pick an outfit when I'm going to be out for a while, or traveling or walking a lot. I've learned that nothing can ruin my time quite like blisters from ill-fitting shoes or feeling cold and wishing I had a jacket. So make lots of mistakes, but don't make the same one twice.

Prompt: Write down a memorable mistake and what you learned from it.

_____

_____

_____

_____

_____

_____

_____

_____

_____

_____

34 Everyone should have a personal cause, something they hope to leave behind.

I ask every close friend and family member this question, "What is your personal cause?" Mine is youth equality and empowerment, my husband's is the environment, my brother's is homelessness, my sister-in-law's is mental health. Think of an issue that really breaks your heart or pulls on your heartstrings that you can contribute to in your time here.

Prompt: What is a cause close to your heart?

_____

_____

_____

_____

Prompt: What are some ways you can contribute to it and change things for generations to come?

_____

_____

_____

_____

35   With only a little light, the moon can show us so much.

Have you ever noticed how you can see the whole moon, even if it's not all exposed or providing light? I've looked up before and noticed this, that you can faintly see the full circle even when the moon is not technically full. Appreciate the parts of the moon that are not quite visible; it's a great visual reminder of unrealized potential, just waiting for the right moment to shine.

Prompt: What is currently unrealized or unrecognized about you and just waiting for its moment to shine?

_____

_____

_____

_____

_____

_____

_____

2 TIME

Remember that while you sleep, the world is working on your tomorrow.

When I was twenty-three, I spent my free time longing for a lot of things: a new job, more real friendships with people in my city, and a boyfriend. I stressed about these things and sometimes let them affect my health by way of poor sleep, poor eating, too much comparison, or too much wine. As I turned twenty-four, many of these things started to change. My brother and one of my best friends moved to my city, and I then moved in with that best friend. I met a guy in my best friend's business school class who became my boyfriend. Months later, I found a new job I was passionate about and made more authentic friendships there. By twenty-five, everything I had cried about and lost sleep over at twenty-three had changed. I don't say this to brag or for you to expect that exact same two-year timeline to happen for you. I say this because it's important to recognize that one event led to another and things happened that I never could have predicted or anticipated. I want you to meet your uncertainties with optimism and trust. There is a lot you can do to affect your own happiness, and I by no means want you to sit passively on the sidelines. But remember that you are not the only one creating the events of your days; God and the whole universe are involved, working every second to unfold your life.

It doesn't take long to learn that the world is working while you sleep. One glimpse of your email or the news when you wake up in the morning can teach you that. Once I fully accepted this concept, my appreciation and my respect for the notion of time increased. I discovered lessons about slowing down, staying out until one a.m., spending the weekend outdoors, waiting, and making history. These are all lessons in time, the common denominator that brings us all together. We act as though we can "make time," but we can't, it's already been set for us. Minutes, hours, days, years, seasons . . . in this chapter you'll learn how to best use and remember the segments that will become your lifetime.

1 Once you start flying, you have to put in a lot of hours and energy to stay up there.

A mentor of mine is semi-retired, and upon retirement, took up flying. He told me about his lessons and all of the practice time he was putting in, and he said something close to the line above. He's so right. Once you get airborne, the work is just beginning. You have to put in even more time and energy to stay flying. It's the perfect metaphor for success: once you get to the top, then the hard work of maintaining your high-flying status really begins.

2 This too shall pass. It's true.

This line is something I hear people say often. Whether you are in a tough personal season, sick, or just not a fan of a current trend, you may hear this phrase from someone in response to your struggle: "This too shall pass." And I'm here as proof that it's true. The first person I ever heard this from was my grandmother, who used to say, "All through the Bible it says that 'it came to pass,' never that it came to stay." An ancient text tells stories of plague and famine and many other tragedies that came to pass. And in our modern world, I've been through sickness, heartbreak, and bad jobs, and I've come out on the other side. Whatever you are going through right now, remind yourself that it won't be forever.

3   Change is constant. Shape it, implement it, learn from it, and then repeat.

4   Stay up late to watch the Olympics.

I've always admired how the Olympic Games, which are characterized by such extreme effort, also so effortlessly connect us all. When we strike up a conversation at work about a surprising finish or recount the story of an incredible human triumph at our dinner table, it becomes clear that the Olympics don't just bring athletes from every continent together; they have a way of bringing us all a little closer too.

By 2012, technology had expanded in such a way that we could see clips or results live, before the Games aired on prime time. I still stayed up late each night to witness things like Michael Phelps becoming the most decorated Olympian of all time and to see a band of young teenage women win gold for the United States in gymnastics. People train their entire lives to compete in events that may last only seconds. And on top of that, it only happens every two years. Be sure to watch.

5   Today, you're younger than you're ever going to be.

6 Always spend weekends in November outdoors.

Depending on where you live, November might not be the best time to be outdoors, but when I wrote this down, I lived in Atlanta, Georgia. In November, every leaf was at its best and every weekend brought the most beautiful and invigorating weather. So, whatever the "November" is in your location, appreciate it and maximize it.

7 You won't always be able to stay out until one a.m. on a Monday night. Do it while you can.

At the age of twenty-two, I was at my first job. I loved it and took it seriously, and I was strict with myself about doing great work and building a great reputation. That meant arriving at the office on time, in optimal condition, and therefore going to bed at a good time. But I was also twenty-two, trying to make new friends, meet a boyfriend, and also just have a good time. My roommate and some friends invited me to a show at a nearby bar, and the act everyone wanted to see wasn't supposed to start until ten p.m. I wanted to be a good friend and I wanted to have a good time and so I went. We drank lots of beers and we danced from ten p.m. until one a.m., and it was so fun.

The next morning, I was tired and my head hurt a little bit behind my eyes, but I still made it to work on time. I discovered an important part of adulthood: You can have a great time and also be great at your job. It takes balance, and you have to experiment with balance in order to find it. I also realized that one day I'd hopefully have a child and more responsibilities and that now was the time to stay out late on a Monday night. I don't recommend that you do it every Monday night, but definitely do it and enjoy it while you can.

8   Ten minutes of undivided attention is worth more than an hour of divided attention.

9   Make time for yourself. The activities you enjoy on a holiday are indeed things you can do every day.

Don't save reading, drinking coffee outside, hiking, doing yoga, or experimenting in the kitchen for your days off. Make time for what relaxes and refreshes you on a "regular" day and it will be a little bit more "yours."

10   Don't wish your days away, no matter what is at the end of your week or month.

"I can't wait to see you!" or "I can't wait for this week to be over!" These are sentiments you might express to a loved one or a friend as you share your plans for the weekend ahead. I've spent all of my adult life separated by geographic distance from people I loved. My parents, a long-distance boyfriend, my best friends. I've had a lot of long weekend visits and big reunion trips to look forward to, and I know it's very easy to wish days away if you have a visit, trip, or other big adventure planned in the future. You find yourself looking ahead and forget to be right here, in the moment you are in. There is greatness in each of your days that you can't just wish away while you eagerly await what is to come. Time goes by fast enough; it doesn't need us to speed it along by wishing it away.

11 Make your evenings feel longer and more important than your workdays.

It took a while to learn this one. Work was it for me during my first few working years. My day consisted of waking up, eating breakfast, and working. But when I met the man who is now my husband, we started making plans for dinners, concerts, and movies in the hours after work. I began to see the life in the day beyond the eight to ten hours I was putting in at the office. The life of your day is not just your workday; it's every minute you are awake. Stop thinking life equals work or a certain set of standard hours and start thinking of all the greatness each day can hold.

12   We now live in a world where if a brand doesn't have a size extra small, they'll likely make one for you.

I worked for an organization with thirty thousand members, and each received a T-shirt. Thus, this organization had a large contract to be won by a T-shirt provider and screen printer. We were once in conversations with a potential partner who was eager to earn our business, but didn't offer a size extra small, which made up a significant number of our membership. We voiced this concern and the vendor said they would start making a size extra small just for us. Our parents didn't live in this world; their time was much different. If they wanted a size XS and someone didn't have it, our parents would say, "okay, I guess I'm a small then." Or "I'll make this size work." This really is an enlightened and fortunate time to be alive. Appreciate that we have so many more options than our parents did; don't take your options for granted. And recognize that even among all the options you have to consider, a generation will come after you that will likely have even more.

13   Sometimes, you figure it out close to the end.

You could learn this one on vacation, on a long run, or while working on a project. It takes time to become familiar with systems, directions, and surroundings. I've been on trips where we kept forgetting where we were supposed to turn, but finally got it on day four of a five-day trip. I've lived in a house where I consistently hit the wrong light switch for the light over the stairs and finally committed the right one to memory only six weeks before I moved out. And many times, I've been out on a run and felt like I'd just hit my stride as I was moving into the last mile. In short, I've discovered that I often gain the confidence and clarity to remember something or get the hang of it when I almost won't need to do it anymore. This isn't true of everything in life, but it's happened to me enough for me to recite this lesson aloud many times.

14   It's okay to just stop and lie in the grass with your dog.

15   You probably think the time before now was the glory days. Before you know it, now will be the glory days.

If you're in your early twenties, you might be looking back at your college years and thinking they were your glory days. If you are in your early thirties with a small baby at home, you might be looking back at when you slept in past seven a.m. and went out to dinner after six p.m.—oh, those were the days. Soon you'll be moved on to a new phase, whatever it might be for you, and the day and moment you are in right now will be one you look back on and wish to experience just one more time. When you had free time to sit down and journal, when you could linger over a cup of coffee and a book or sit quietly with your thoughts and someone else's. There's something glorious about each phase and stage. Don't wait until you have to look back on it to notice the goodness of what you are experiencing right now.

16   Remind yourself that this is temporary, all of it.

Even the time and decisions you think are permanent or forever . . . unfortunately, they are not.

17   Try not to talk about the memory while you are still making it. Just enjoy it.

How often do you talk about how amazing or unforgettable an experience is while it's still happening? My mom was visiting me and my brother in Atlanta and we were out to dinner celebrating her birthday. My mom said, "Oh, this is going to be the sweetest memory," while we were very much still in the middle of what would hopefully become a memory. You may not realize it, but saying those thoughts out loud can alter the event or moment and may change the way you will remember it. I know we can recognize when something is so good or sweet. It's a gift to feel these moments and know they are special, but to make a true memory, try to stay in the moment.

18   Spend your twenties exploring, and don't settle (into a job, relationship, or home) until it's really good.

19   Don't wait for the things you want.

If patience is a virtue, being bold and taking ownership are virtues too. I believe you should passionately pursue the desires of your heart. Take a moment to imagine how you want to spend the rest of your life, who you will be with and what you will spend your days doing. If you are not currently with that person or on your way to doing that kind of work or action every day, then quickly make some changes and go after those things. I made a big geographic move because I knew I wanted to be next to a certain person for the rest of my life and I couldn't wait to see if we'd end up in the same place later. I also made a risky move to leave a job because every night as I drove home, I envisioned myself doing a different kind of work for the rest of my working days. Our life is indeed short and finite; we don't even know how much time we have. So don't wait for the things you want to happen to you. Do whatever is in your power to work toward them now.

20   Things happen when they are meant to, even if the order doesn't make sense to you right away.

21   Spend time with kids, the elderly, or others you may not interact with in your day-to-day life. It's good for your soul and your brain.

Make time in your life to volunteer. It's important to give of your resource of time. Sure, you can donate to organizations financially, but I've found that giving of your time can be a greater investment. Yes, this chapter is about time, and you might feel that yours is limited, or you might reply that I mentioned in the beginning of this chapter that we can't "make" time. So find a way to dedicate some of your time to someone else. Give yourself an additional challenge to find an organization or demographic that is different from where or whom you usually dedicate your time to in your home or work life.

My personal cause is youth empowerment. I strongly believe that every child should have the same chance, regardless of their circumstances. I also really love sports and the opportunities they provided me as a child and an adult. I volunteer as a coach for a local Girls on the Run chapter, teaching elementary-age girls about their limitless potential through the sport of running. It allows me the chance to be outside two afternoons a week, running, walking, and teaching a curriculum based on building self-esteem. It has been one of the most rewarding and enriching experiences of my adult life, and I wish it could somehow be my full-time gig. You might not find as compatible of an organization as I did, but at least attempt to in the hope that you do.

22 Don't forget: Making history is a gift. By preserving our most important ideas and moments, we get to relive them.

We grow up learning to celebrate history. Certain months and dates are dedicated to important moments in the life of our nation and the world. Our own lives are made up of these same momentous and celebratory occasions. Each day we're making history, and it's up to us to think of it that way. Consider, are you making moments that are worth celebrating? How are you recording them? I believe it's a gift to have lived and learned, and to be able to look back at what was and how we've grown. Whether you recognize it or not, you are already making history. Now it's time that you make ways for it to be remembered and celebrated too.

23 Read old books. The stories are just as exciting, the language is just older.

24   Try things when you are young, before you know how to be nervous.

Nerves grow with you. Have you ever noticed just how unaware children are of the water temperature of an inviting, yet cold, lake or ocean? They run and leap right in! They don't know to be nervous, just like they don't know the water is freezing. So take more leaps while you are young, before you've learned things that might make you nervous, and if you are already a parent, encourage your children to do the same.

25   Don't wait in long lines for mediocre things.

In my adult years, I've seen way too many people wait over one and a half hours for a very average brunch. Our culture has become obsessed with obsessing over items and experiences simply because they have a long line or a waiting list. The scarcity model and its marketing tactic really seem to work on us. But I believe that life is too short to spend it waiting in long lines. Unless you can honestly say, "This is the best _____ I've ever had or seen in my life," don't wait in a long line for it.

There are few things that I've stood in a long line for that proved to be worth it. I waited in a long line to see Michelangelo's David statue, which mesmerized me, and I waited in a long line for the best pork chop I've ever had in my life, both of which were in Florence, Italy. I've also stood in a long line for the best breakfast sandwich I've ever had in my life, here in my current hometown of Annapolis, Maryland. But I've generally stood outside of too many restaurants waiting way too long for average food. I also once stood in a line for three hours for a themed pop-up bar because it was something friends of mine wanted to do. That night, I swore to myself I'd never stand in a long line for an underwhelming experience again. There are plenty of places you can get breakfast food. I love a good, average breakfast spot with no wait. And sure, it might not be quite as good as the one with the really long line, but with the time you saved, you'll have a head start on the next best thing.

26   Take time to reflect.

In the same way you budget your financial resources, you should budget your time. Save some for yourself. In your twenties it's so easy to get caught up in motion, always on the run; looking for fun, for the next best thing, and for the answers to your biggest questions. It's important to stop and take time out of every day to recount your proudest and happiest moments. At the end of the day, set aside time, even just a few minutes, to reflect on what made you smile or when you felt proud. Not only will it boost your happiness and your confidence, it's simply a good habit to form.

27   Do what you know you won't regret later.

No one likes regret, and I've discovered that all regret is not equal. Some regret stays with me longer than others, and the same may be true for you. Sure, there have been some decisions or actions in my life that I've simply wished I'd done differently: *I wish I hadn't done both tequila and Fireball shots in the same night,* as it had me throwing up and in bed until four p.m. the next day. Or *I wish I had responded differently to that interview question,* as I proceed to replay the interview in my mind while trying to go to sleep. Then there are others that I've lamented about in a life-altering way, and they seem to come back up yearly. *I think I should have stayed in that job longer. Was leaving it the right decision for my career?* Or *I miss a certain friend and her wisdom. How could I have done a better job showing up for her and nourishing our relationship so that we didn't lose touch?*

I mentioned earlier in this chapter that I consider myself a recovering dweller, and that moniker is relevant to this lesson too. Take it from someone who knows the topic of ruminating well: When you are met with uncertainty and indecisiveness, try not only to think about the decision at hand, but also about which outcome you as an individual are more likely to hold on to in a negative way. If there is an option that you don't know is the right move for right away, but you know in the long run it will relieve your mind, then use that as the driver to make your decision.

28 No one warns you about the feelings of your late twenties.

Take it from a person who definitely didn't see it coming. I feel that no one warned me about the feelings I encountered in my late twenties. There are all of these lessons and cautions for sixteen, eighteen, twenty-five, and thirty. But what about twenty-eight? At that age, I found myself thinking, *Why didn't anyone warn me that this crossroads lay ahead?* The feelings during this time of my life were unexpected and intricate, made up of the weight of trying not to disappoint my twenty-one-year-old self while also making decisions that my forty-year-old self could live with. At this age, you might find yourself thinking about who you were, who you are, and who you want to be all at the same time.

As an early twentysomething, I asked myself questions like, *Is this all there is?* or *Is what I'm working on good for my career?* As I aged, the weight of the questions and feelings got heavier. As a late twentysomething, I asked myself questions like *Is what I'm working on good for the world and sustainable for my future? Is this fulfilling enough to be my forever?* or *Is it possible to consider being a mom in this career?* This was the particular crossroads I came to earlier than I expected. I was twenty-nine when the reality sank in that only one female in my department with "senior" in her title also answered to Mom, and work/life balance seemed impossible for me to ever achieve.

The crossroads might not be twenty-eight or twenty-nine for you, but there may come a time when you become concerned not only with what's good for the world and for your future but also for your children (or future children) while still making good on the expectations you set for yourself.

Consider yourself warned, it can be a heavy load to carry. If you haven't gotten to your late twenties yet, be proactive in taking the time to recognize the things you've accomplished instead of only dwelling on the ones that you haven't yet. Also, take a look around your office or industry. Is there a female superior to you who lives a life you would want to emulate? However, if you, like me, missed the warning and have fully experienced the weight of these questions, know that it's never too late to evaluate what's important to you now and make changes. After all, you're likely only about a third of the way through this incredible life you've been gifted.

29   Make more days your favorite days.

At a New Year's Eve celebration, a family member once asked, "What was your favorite day of the year?" I loved this question, as it required everyone in attendance to reflect on the memories of the year, a favorite practice of mine at this time of year, and to also then voice what was important to us, what we prioritized and prized. That particular year it seemed I must have prized peace, adventure, and seclusion, since I recounted my favorite day as one on a vacation in Maine, a place I had never been before. That day, I went out in a kayak by myself with nothing but a water bottle, a snack, and a book. I rowed out into the middle of the water and then put my paddle in the boat, put my feet up, and just drifted away.

Prompt: What was your favorite day of the last year, and how can you make a greater number of your days just like that one?

_____

_____

_____

_____

_____

_____

30 You have twenty-four hours each day. Use them to make yourself happy.

Twenty-four hours is actually a lot of hours. Imagine working for twenty-four hours straight or doing something physically strenuous for twenty-four hours. If you did, you'd realize just how long of a time that really is. So when you think about and plan for the day ahead, think about allotting time for the things that bring you the most joy. Over the years I've seen many magazine publications ask celebrities, "If you could spend twenty-four hours doing anything with no limitations, what would it be?" Now imagine that same opportunity for yourself.

Prompt: How would you most like to spend twenty-four hours?

_____

_____

_____

_____

_____

_____

What do you think this reveals about your priorities?

_____

_____

_____

_____

_____

31   If you take the time to slow down, things will slow down.

"An object at rest tends to stay at rest unless acted upon by an outside force." This might be one of the only things from grade school science that I actually committed to memory, and I'm glad I did because it's the first thing that came to mind when I sat down with this lesson. In the same way that something stays at rest until an action sets it in motion, something stays hurried or fast until an action slows it down. I learned this lesson while working for a very fast-paced company; I used to pack snacks in my backpack, as some days I literally ate "lunch" while speed-walking to my next meeting. It was fast and, trust me, I did genuinely love the hustle. But I also learned that if one person took the time to slow down a meeting, it allowed everyone in attendance the chance to let their shoulders drop and pay closer attention. Or if I slowed down from a sprint to the printer and took my time, I gave my brain a moment of clarity to rejuvenate. Urgency begets more urgency. Sometimes things might actually be urgent, but many times they are not, so when it's possible and necessary, take the time to slow things down.

Prompt: When was the last time you intentionally tried to slow down and took your time over a meal, giving a presentation, or exploring a new relationship? What did you notice that you possibly didn't have the time to notice before?

_____

_____

_____

_____

_____

_____

_____

_____

_____

_____

_____

32 Use December 31 as a day to reflect on your year, not to try to accomplish all of your year-end goals.

I tried this once. I woke up on the last day of the year with an overwhelming desire to fulfill two of my goals for the year I hadn't gotten to yet: volunteering for a new organization and participating in an extreme sport. I tried to pack it all into one day, and when I couldn't, I felt deflated and discouraged about what I had accomplished. It's possible that as a society we place way too much pressure on crossing the December 31 to January 1 threshold "successfully." After the experience of waiting until the last minute and putting unnecessary pressure on myself, I learned to be intentional all year long. I encourage you to set goals and set aside time to accomplish those goals throughout the year, so you can spend the last day of the year reflecting on what you've done and not researching what you should do—or regretting what you haven't done.

Prompt: What are your personal and professional goals for the year ahead?

_____

_____

_____

_____

33 Honor your first impressions and listen to your gut, but also be willing to accept that people aren't always their true selves initially.

I'm married to someone who, for many months, I said was "just a friend," who I may have even once described as a "convenient companion." I cringe and smile with my teeth gritted a little any time I say that out loud. My first impression was that he was a guy's guy, fun, good at sports and finance, but that my relationship with him wouldn't be a long-term one. I was looking for someone with more depth, into art and music, interested in long conversations about life's big questions, and he kept it pretty surface-level at first.

As I spent more time with him, though, I learned I was actually wrong about him. He turned out to be quite a Renaissance man. I learned that he painted and built furniture and could play the piano. I also learned that while he's often in a state of silent reflection and doesn't talk nearly as much as I do, he can go deep in a philosophical conversation. As we grew closer, he shared that he had walls up at first, as he wasn't in a place where he was looking for a serious relationship. And so I learned an important lesson, that while my first impression might have been an accurate read, it wasn't the truth. It's good to trust your gut, but make some allowance for grace, since what you've perceived might not always be reality.

Prompt: Was your first impression of someone ever wrong? How was it wrong, and what did you learn?

_____

_____

_____

_____

_____

_____

_____

_____

_____

_____

_____

34   Make the most of what you are given and play your hand.

My family played a lot of cards growing up, specifically a lot of rummy or rummy 500. It's very easy to get into the habit of complaining about being dealt a bad hand, but don't do it. Don't seek pity when it's bad, and don't boast when it's good. In all my days of playing, I can attest that the game can change very quickly. Just play the cards you have, and you will get new ones.

Prompt: Has your situation or favor ever changed quickly from good to bad or bad to good? What did you learn from the feelings of each and the shift in between?

_____

_____

_____

_____

_____

_____

_____

35 It's possible that things aren't the same because you aren't the same.

This one can be hard to accept. In my mid-twenties, I moved to a city where I knew no one except for my boyfriend, leaving a job I loved and family behind. Finding a new job that satisfied me as much as my former one was hard, and so were making new friends and building a life that felt like mine and not my boyfriend's. I'd had such an easy time of it before, but now nothing was coming together as it had for me in the past. I wondered daily why I was struggling so much. My mom reminded me, "Maybe it doesn't feel the same because you aren't the same as you used to be, either." She was right. I had changed and I needed to keep changing. Every next stage of our lives requires us to grow and bring an advanced, different version of ourselves to the table. So the next time you question why something isn't the same, don't just look outward for an answer, look inward as well.

Prompt: What has changed about you since this time last year?

_____

_____

_____

_____

_____

36   Now and then you will miss being twenty-one.

It might be, but hopefully not, for the raging social life you had at twenty-one. For me, I often miss the young business-woman I was at that age: eager and naïve, at the beginning of her career and imagining what work life would be like when she would be twenty-nine. I miss how everything was unknown to me at twenty-one. There's nothing wrong with this longing. One day, I know I will miss being thirty and fifty and sixty-five, and I hope you will too.

Prompt: What has been your favorite age to date and why? What do you miss most about the way you thought then?

_____

_____

_____

_____

_____

_____

3 LOVE

Don't go looking for love, go looking for things you love to do.

The great love story of my life begins in a wide-open field in a park in the city of Atlanta, filled with tables, pop-up tents, and beer taps. I met my husband at a beer festival. I wasn't looking for love, I was looking for a fun time doing some day drinking with my girlfriends and hopefully discovering a new favorite craft beer. In fact, I may have been so focused on myself, my provisions for the potential rain downpour in the forecast, and my friends that I failed to notice what I now see in hindsight as the first actual touchpoints of my relationship with my husband and how our relationship began. In a large group of friends and acquaintances of friends, my now-husband sat next to me on the way to the festival, our knees and ribs touching as we crammed into the backseat of a taxi van. He conveniently wanted to go to all of the beer tents I was going to, and later in the day, when it started to rain, he asked, "Can I put my cell phone in your Ziploc bag?" My attention to the forecast had paid off. I do love a good daytime festival, and I didn't notice many of my future husband's attentions at first, because I was doing something I loved doing with a few people I already loved, not looking for love.

Beer festivals may not be your thing, but start thinking about and identifying the things you love to do. Maybe that's joining a running club because you love to run and exercise, going to painting classes because you want to improve your art skills, or attending an industry networking event because you care about nurturing your career. This is a great time in life to work on finding a new community or a new hobby, to focus on yourself.

Instead of just focusing on myself, I spent much of my early twenties longing to be in a serious relationship, often thinking too much about how and where I'd find my life partner. Would he be the guy I serendipitously rode in the office building elevator with many mornings, or the guy behind me in the checkout line at the grocery store? The idea here is that if you find yourself critically reviewing and interviewing every person you come across as a potential candidate for the job of spending the rest of your lives together, you aren't likely to find someone, and the search can become both exhausting and depressing. However, if you dedicate your energy and resources to enriching your life by finding new hobbies, growing the ones you love, and strengthening your existing relationships with people you already care about, you are more likely to find your way into a romantic relationship with someone you love and care about.

Whether you are just married or don't ever plan to be, or you are tired of swiping left and looking for a partner left

and right, this chapter, and my own romantic trials and trib-
ulations, highlight that at all stages, action—chasing, changing, losing, pursuing, and choosing—is necessary for love.
So let your first action be that you are getting busy doing
something you love to do. Running, painting, planting,
exploring, or whatever it may be. An added bonus is that if
you find someone you love while doing something you love,
you'll likely already have something in common. Maybe you
ran a race together, maybe you both prefer a specific type of
art supply, or have complementary business skills and find
yourselves working on a freelance project together. Or, in
my case, maybe you both love a good hoppy IPA and connect because you both like to take good care of your things.
Hopefully you'll learn that this word we've been told is love
doesn't always look, sound, or feel the way we imagine.

1   Either start asking people out, or start accepting the people who ask you out.

One of my very best friends gets the credit for this line and for teaching me this lesson. I was single, in my early twenties, and, as I mentioned, I was very eager to be in a more serious relationship. However, I didn't like any of the people pursuing me at the time. I would find myself complaining that they weren't my type or worried that the current candidates were all I could attract. But I also wasn't putting in the effort to pursue anyone different. Thankfully, I had a girlfriend who brought me a good truth: If you don't like your situation, do something about it.

2   A relationship doesn't have to mean anything, it just has to teach us something.

The person you are dating might not be "the one" in the same way your current job might not be your career. In fact, you may go in a completely different direction in terms of the type of partner you're seeking, but you have to explore and gain experience to know what you're looking for in the first place. Understanding that what you're doing right now isn't forever is vitally important. A person doesn't have to be "perfect" for you in order to be a worthwhile investment of your time and energy. You can still learn so much from the experience. What matters is that you're always learning: about love, about others, and about the type of partnership that makes you your best self.

3   There will be days when you are stuck
inside all day. Make sure you like the person
you are stuck with.

4   Be careful with your heart; don't let it look
back.

Beware of the late-night text and the reunion dinner when
you and an ex-boyfriend or former partner are both home
for the holidays or in the same city for work. These are dangerous activities to partake in with a former partner. It will
always be hard to decipher nostalgia from true undeniable
feelings. You may come home from time together and find
yourself longing for what you had. But what you are likely
feeling is comfort and familiarity, not compatibility and
destiny. So be careful with your heart and don't put yourself
in these situations. They can be both painful and painfully
confusing.

5   The thing about casual dating is that at
some point it will either stop, or stop being
casual. You have to be okay with either
outcome.

As a young twentysomething, I spent a period of time dating
casually, as I believe everyone should do at some point in
their twenties. I even went on two dates with two different
men in the same week, which felt like a rite of passage into

adulthood. At age twenty-four, I consistently casually dated the same guy for a little while. We had agreed on the level and definition of our time spent together, which eventually made its way up the hierarchy all the way to, "exclusive but not in a relationship." We were happily spending our time together in the present without worrying too much about the future, as the guy in this situation wasn't going to live in the same city as me much longer.

I was having fun. I was learning things about myself and what I wanted in a relationship. Like how important ambition is to me as a trait in a partner. Or how I like to plan things, but it's really nice to let someone else take the reins and surprise me with a date night. I often said aloud, "It doesn't have to mean anything, it just has to teach us something." However, as we continued to spend all of our free time together, I began to realize that I was becoming more attached. I felt some walls come down when we made plans for things in the future or when we went to his business school events as a couple with other known couples. And it turned out I wasn't the only one. One day as we sat outside having a drink, he pulled his chair right next to mine and said to me, "Let's go all in on this." Just like that we went from a casual dating relationship to what then became a serious long-distance one.

Casual dating is great. It's fun, as long as you can keep yourself straight and honest. There are only two ways that casual dating comes to an end. It will either stop completely, leaving you on your own again, or it will stop being casual, leaving you seriously attached to the other person. There's no harm done as long as you are truly okay no matter which way it goes.

6 The only thing worse than being heartbroken is being heartbroken and homeless.

Don't move in with someone unless you are very sure about the relationship or very sure you have a backup place to live.

7 Be with someone who can handle the bumps in the road.

I mean this practically and metaphorically. While on a vacation in Costa Rica, my boyfriend (now husband) had to drive over rough, flooded, and poorly lit roads. To give you a visual, there was a time when we had to swerve off the road in the middle of the night to avoid a large bull, and another time when I had to get out of the car to measure the level of the water to make sure we could get through. He handled it all like a champ. He's also handled the rough terrain of my headspace through the years as I've soul-searched or made a hard decision to shift my career. You need to be with someone who doesn't stop short, turn around, or say they'll pick you up on the other side, but who is excited to take on the obstacles with you.

8   When choosing a partner, find an addition, not a completion.

It's important to be fully comfortable with yourself. The idea of saying, "You complete me," (credit to Tom Cruise in *Jerry Maguire*) to someone is actually quite dangerous. You don't need to be "completed." The best relationships are those made up of two people who are each just fine on their own, but enhance each other's best qualities.

9   Leave space for your future family and friends to enter your life.

Don't work so hard that you don't allow time or space for your future family and friends to enter your life. My brother took a new job in a new city and he loved to work. He worked at his job all day and did his own freelance work all night. He would then complain about not making any friends or meeting any potential dating interests. But you have to create space for these things. If you're working too hard to meet any people at all then there's a very slim chance you'll make friends or be able to find a life partner.

10   "We accept the love we think we deserve."

If you've never read or watched *The Perks of Being a Wallflower* by Stephen Chbosky, do it. It's an iconic story about coming of age and gaining self-knowledge. I heard the line quoted above in the movie, and it stuck with me. Sometimes people in our lives will choose the wrong people to date, people who don't treat them the way they should be treated. It's possible that's all they've known, or that it's the best they think they can do. Make sure the people in your life know real love and know that they deserve the best.

11 Not everyone has had the same experiences you have had.

You already know this to be true about life, but it's true in love too. We're not all working from the same foundation of relationship experience, so remember to give each other some space and some grace. I was in a serious relationship for five years, and was then in a relationship with someone whose longest relationship had only ever been about one year. We approached things differently because our comfort level in a long-term romantic relationship was different. I also dated the same person through almost all of college, which creates a very different background from someone who possibly didn't have a relationship in college. I didn't go on a lot of group road trips or have any college one-night stands; I went on a lot of nice dinner dates instead. The point is, you can't assume that people know how you feel or what you are talking about. We're all coming at things with different past experiences and learned expectations.

12   Choosing a life partner is like getting to pick first in kickball.

You get the first pick, it's your choice. Don't let anyone make you feel differently. And most importantly, make sure you pick a great team.

13   If someone wants to see you, they'll make it happen.

14   You can't change the shape of a piece to force it into your puzzle.

I went through a hard breakup coming out of college. The relationship ended maturely and for a noble reason: religious differences. Neither of us was willing to change our stance or commitment to our different religions. It was a hard breakup because I still cared for this person, and there had been no hurtful affair or unexpected offense, just the inability to change our minds and hearts. I learned that as painful as it can be to break up with someone, you just can't force something that doesn't fit. Like a puzzle, the pieces (and in this case the people) are what they are, a distinct and intentional shape. You can't really manipulate or modify puzzle pieces, and if you did, the pieces wouldn't stay together and the whole thing would fall apart.

15   Some people can stay in your heart, but not in your life.

16   Love your neighbor as yourself.

Have you ever really stopped and thought about the meaning of this line? We grow up hearing this as children, maybe in church or as the golden rule in school. As an adult I learned to process this line for what it really means; to do for others and hope for others in the same way I do for myself. I'm still not very good at this when it comes to my literal neighbors; in fact, I confess that I barely know my current next-door neighbor, but I'm working toward it, and eager to be in community with them. But this saying applies to more than just our actual next-door neighbors, it's about all of the people alongside us as we do life. I'm constantly working to know them, love them, and treat them in the ways that I want to be treated.

17   People give and sacrifice in different ways. It isn't always one for one.

18 "Blessed are the moments in life when the decision is clear."

This was the first line of a poem that my husband wrote on a notecard and gave to me when he asked me to be his wife. (He'd heard it somewhere and copied it down to share with me, but neither of us has been able to track down an actual source for it since.) Once I started reading the poem and noticed him in my peripheral, getting down on one knee, I started to black out a little bit. I had to re-read the poem, and I don't think I heard anything he said. But fortunately, this first line, the one I read the most times, stuck with me, and it summarized the way I felt so well. It was a blessing to be so very sure of my response to the question he asked me. I said "Yes" before he even opened or gave me the ring box. And I recorded this line as a lesson because it is a great guide. No matter the question at hand, whether it's asking yourself, "Is it time to move on?," or if someone else is asking you, "Would you like to move in?," the moments in love when your decisions are clear are real blessings, even if they might not feel that way at the time.

19 Marriage is so much more than the details of a wedding day.

My wedding took place in 2016, and I'm glad I got married when I did, since I feel that the wedding industry has exploded in an even bigger way since then. The expectations that have been brought on for destination weddings, weekend-long affairs, late-night food trucks, dessert displays and photo walls, all thanks to Instagram, seem like a lot to take on. I'm by no means dissing these components, and I happily attend extravagant weddings, but I've known a few too many brides who have gotten very caught up in all of this over the last few years. I was sharing wedding stories and advice with a younger bride-to-be and discovered myself saying the line above. Of course, this is one of those lines that can only be brought about by the experience of marriage. But your marriage *is* so much more than the details of a wedding day. One is only for a day, and the other is hopefully for the rest of your life.

I like to think that's why there is a separate word for the event and the union and it's not called your "marriage day." I recognize that in the same way marriage isn't for everyone, weddings aren't either. But if you find yourself at this milestone and next stage of your life, don't forget to focus on your marriage and your union with another person in the midst of all of your planning. After the day is done, when all of the floral arrangements have been given away and all of the donuts have been eaten, that's when the most important stuff begins.

20   A great fire must always be tended to.

I'm not much of a fire builder. I'm happy to sit fireside with a drink or to participate in the festivity of making a s'more, but I'm never going to be the first one who volunteers to make the fire. Thankfully, my brother and my husband both love to build fires. They like to place the logs in a certain pattern, to light it in just the right spot, to continuously prod the wood to grow the flame. In the times when they haven't been present while I'm in the presence of a fire, I've realized that you can't just light a match and walk away. When building a bonfire, a fire in a fireplace, or a fire in your heart for a person or a thing, remember that fire requires your attention and care, both so it doesn't go wild and so it doesn't go out.

21   Share the joys of your relationship with friends just as much as you share your concerns.

I was gathered in my living room in Atlanta, with my room-mate and two of our other girlfriends. We'd just had a girls' night dinner and were all cozy on couches in the living room, talking about our relationships or recent dates. As I listened to my friends and also to myself, I realized that with our closest friends we seem more likely to share our hesitations and doubts about our romantic relationships and encounters than we do our joys and excitement.

This occurred to me as I found myself concerned at a friend's decision to become more serious with someone who I wasn't positive was a great fit for her. We are often unfair to our friends by only describing our dating and relation-ship woes, leaving them with doubt and concern. Please do continue to share the stuff you are unsure of or want your best friends' buy-in on. But also share the good stuff, so they know there *is* good stuff and they can celebrate the relationship with you too.

22 Be content with quiet. You'll be a better person and a better partner for it.

23 If you get married, never stop dating your spouse.

24 For everything you lost or left behind, you will gain or be given another thing.

I moved for love, and when I did, I left behind a city I loved and many other treasures, including a great job, my brother, and one of my very best friends. It's hard to recognize this at first or to keep this perspective as you are moving on and growing, but while you are losing and leaving behind, you are also gaining in return. Over time in my new city, I gained a life partner, unparalleled professional peers and mentors, a tight-knit church community, and new friends. And while the experience I've shared is specific to moving to a new city, moving on in relationships is much the same. When you find yourself sad, mourning the loss of someone or a certain aspect of a relationship, take note of the additions to your life that might not have happened if you had not made the change.

Prompt: What is something that you feel like you've lost in a relationship or because of one? Can you look closer to recognize something you gained too?

_____

_____

_____

_____

_____

25   Be foolishly in love.

Dancing in the middle of the street, staying on the phone until you've practically fallen asleep, retrieving love notes tucked under the windshield wiper of your car, phone calls received minutes after you've left to simply say "I miss you." These things sound like they are out of a romantic comedy, but I can attest, foolish love does exist in real life. Everyone should get to experience being with someone who makes them feel this way. Don't settle for anyone less special than that.

Prompt: When was the last time you fell foolishly in love with someone or something? What did you do that made you realize it?

_____

_____

_____

_____

_____

_____

26 Heartache is a real thing.

You'll recognize that feeling in your heart when you've felt it a time or two. You might say out loud "my heart hurts," and that's the only thing you'll be sure of at the time. That feeling of heartache just might be love. It was for me, but I had no idea at the time. It took me a few more times to recognize it. Pay attention to the moments when "your heart hurts" and see if you can recognize a pattern, too.

Prompt: Is there a feeling you've had more than once, but you don't quite know what it is? What does it feel like and how can you help yourself figure out what it means?

_____

_____

_____

_____

_____

_____

_____

27 Move for love.

When I say that love doesn't always look, sound, or feel like we imagine it does, it's in part because I never imagined that anyone could change my plans. But love did. If you'd told me in college that I would move for a romantic relationship, I would have laughed in your face. My sophomore college roommate and I actually laugh about this still, as we both ended up moving to live in the cities of our significant others, and neither of us could believe we'd done it. Fortunately for both of us, they turned out to be our husbands. Be willing to move for love and don't be ashamed or embarrassed by it. It's a gift to love so strongly that you'd uproot your current life for the potential of what might be in store. And even if it doesn't end the way mine did, I'm confident that God and the universe recognize the act of giving of yourself and that your move will put other things and plans into motion.

Prompt: What circumstances would make you leave a city you love for your partner?

_____

_____

_____

_____

_____

_____

_____

_____

_____

28   When you are in a relationship, test drive a car together. You'll learn a lot about him or her by the features he or she is interested in.

The decisions someone makes can tell you a lot about them. Car buying may be one of the most revealing situations because it involves making decisions about money, preference, and priorities. Do they spend extra money on leather seats and a sunroof or stick with the basic model? Pay attention to the gas mileage or not so much? Plan to buy the car outright, lease it, or finance it? Walk off the lot with it that day or take time to consider before purchasing? These decisions communicate a lot and offer an opportunity to ask questions to help you get to know each other better.

Prompt: Think of someone you know and what their car preferences might say about them. Have they overextended themselves, showing that appearances matter more than financial stability? Do they value practicality or luxury?

_____

_____

_____

_____

_____

29   Give a person a chance for four seasons. Doing so allows you to see them change with each.

Just as flowers and plants change in appearance with each season, human beings change over the course of a year too. I, for one, bloom in the summer/fall and might not be my best self in winter. Implementing this lesson into your life could go more than one way. You may have met someone in their toughest season and be able to learn so many more things about them in the months and seasons that follow. Or it's possible you've met someone while they were peaking, in full bloom, and you might have to watch their petals fall and learn that it may be harder for them to come back to life. If you are dating a person who you are considering as a life partner, or if you've met someone you'd like to date more seriously, know them for all four seasons of a year before making any permanent decisions.

Prompt: How are you different in each season? How have you seen someone else change with the seasons?

_____

_____

_____

_____

_____

_____

30   "You can tell the measure of a man by the company he keeps."

The president of my first advertising agency shared this ancient proverb with me, in the context of describing the types of people she hired or wanted on her team. But I think this quote applies to romantic relationships too. Take note of a new acquaintance's friends or the friends of someone you have recently started dating. You can learn a lot about someone by the people surrounding them or the people they speak of most often.

Prompt: Based only on the people you spend the most time with, what might someone say about the kind of person you are?

_____

_____

_____

_____

_____

_____

31 Everyone has moments of weakness. Pursuing love is not one of those moments. If anything, chasing love and giving of yourself requires more strength.

My brother dropped this one on me over dinner in a barbecue restaurant. I was considering quitting my job and moving to a different city for a guy, and I was torn up inside about what doing so said about me. I thought it made me seem weak. My brother shared the lines above with me, and I encourage you to repeat them to yourself if you are considering moving or changing your path for a loved one. It doesn't make you any less driven or independent. It's actually one of the bravest things you can do.

Prompt: How have you grown as an individual through a relationship with another?

_____

_____

_____

_____

_____

_____

4 WORK

*Creation and destruction often happen
simultaneously.*

It's important to learn this lesson early in your career,
so you don't mourn the loss of too many ideas, roles, or
projects. I was in my first advertising job, working on my
second monthly campaign for a national fast-food chain,
when I discovered that the excitement of a new advertising
campaign and updated creative work meant the end of the
previous one. Even though it was work we had spent a great
deal of time on and been very proud of, it had to come down
to make space for the next promotion. We may not always
realize it, but there is a constant exchange of resources going
on in our lives, particularly when it comes to work.

This idea continued to prove true in other examples
throughout my various jobs. When a company I worked for
went through reorganization and new positions were created
and posted, other positions were eliminated too. When a
business I worked with developed a new system, an old one
was used less often and eventually became obsolete. There's
no tragedy here, just the realization that when something

is being built or prioritized, something else has likely been dismantled or deprioritized in order to make it. And later I realized that not only was this true for job-related events, but also for the very idea of work and its effect on me as a being.

I used to think that work defined me. It's the first question many people ask at a cocktail party, "What do you do?" And it's often a part of our introduction, the next thing we say after our names to identify ourselves. I love to work; I'm someone who identifies with professional success and contribution. So, trust me, I know it can feel natural to think that your work and what you do right now is the most important thing. The thoughts about what you will do next and who you will be, they can be all-consuming. But these discoveries about creation and destruction reveal that work is evolutionary. While we are all busy participating in our crafts, we are also subtly and slowly crafting ourselves. You might prioritize one area of your interest in work and thus shift away from another, whether you even realize it or not. You could focus in on the goal of a new role and let that guide the decisions you make and the relationships you cultivate. You might decide to remove something from your plate or your workload to make space for a new client or a new project you want to do. In each of these scenarios and in each of the career moves you make, you are both doing and undoing at the same time.

Whether you spend your days making a product or making decisions, you are learning to make a living. For those just starting a career or those down the road already following a calling, this chapter shares lessons about confidence, creation, communication, rejection, and balance. In these years of your life, work can feel like the most important part, and that's okay. I spent much of my time in my twenties thinking that work was who I was. It turns out that work doesn't define me, but actually that it has refined me. I've learned to recognize that my identity isn't a reflection of my job or title, but rather that all of the intentional doing (and accompanying undoing) of my career choices has actually molded the person I am today. I hope you can learn to do the same.

1 It's what you bring to the table, not how long you've been sitting at it.

Coincidentally, two companies I was associated with had layoffs on the same day. One was the agency I worked for at the time and the other was the company my dad worked for. My company based their decisions for who stayed and who went on the philosophy, *it doesn't matter if you have been here for years, contribution determines your worth*. And fortunately, I stayed. My dad's company had the opposite mentality. Despite being the highest performer, my dad got let go because, unfortunately, he was the most recent hire. It's frustrating that an organization with that approach still exists. It sends the wrong message. As with anything in life, don't get complacent. Make sure you are bringing your best self to the table and aim to work for organizations that value your contribution over your time clocked in.

2 Don't ask too many people for their opinion. If you do, you'll lose your own.

3 "If you can't explain it simply, you don't understand it well enough."

This quote from Albert Einstein has guided my work in more ways than I could have ever imagined. I wrote it on a Post-it Note and kept it on a bulletin board at my first job, and it has traveled with me to every job since. It's an incredible reminder to know yourself and your craft well. When we fully understand things, we can speak about them clearly and confidently. It's a good test for you to practice when explaining a new concept or theory, or pitching yourself for a role.

4   Work hard; it is noticed. Not working hard is also noticed.

5   Sending them "what you have" always ends badly.

"We need to send something, so let's just send them what we have." I can remember overhearing these words from a superior in my office to a coworker on the other side of my cubicle. These are terrible words to hear; no one wants to be on the sending or receiving end of such a move. In school or at work, you may feel pressure to hold a deadline or submit a draft of a paper or project before it's ready. You may think "I need to send this now, so let's just send this. It's better than nothing." Think again and don't do it, you want to be known as better than "better than nothing."

6   At some point everyone is scared shitless, it's just a matter of who hides it the best.

7 Have the confidence to be humble.

It's easy to bask in the glory of greatness. But it takes a sur-prisingly great deal of work and confidence to be humble when you achieve greatness; to redirect, to reduce your own shine, to relay the credit to someone or something else. In our culture it's quite popular to focus on being seen and known, to want to be a big deal if even to a small number of people. But try to resist this. Do things for other people, not for praise from those people. My hope for you is that you will do great things, but I know that you will also do things that no one cares about or ever even notices. Either way, be humble and stay humble.

8 Your experience will often not match your future desires.

But that's the whole point, right? We should continue to want more than what we've already done in order to grow our career. This, however, was and is always the most frus-trating part of applying for jobs in the beginning of your career: "How can I get consumer research experience if I have to have consumer research experience to get this con-sumer research job?" There are a few ways to minimize this gap: seek additional education, network with people who have the experience you are hoping to gain, offer pro bono work in the area you are hoping to expand to, or ask for new responsibilities at your current job to help you learn the skills in the area where you are lacking.

9   Take the free samples.

Have you ever been to an ice cream shop that has unlimited free samples? Or paid attention to how the paint section has so many color options for you to simply take with you and test out? I recommend that you start your work life with the same mindset: take as many samples as you'd like. You might have to try a variety of different jobs or career paths in order to figure out the best one for you. While you are young, with fewer obligations or costs to worry about, explore as many opportunities as you can in order to figure out what you love to do. Don't worry about wasting time or tasting too many different things. You'll have more to worry about later if you don't take the chances right now, while you can.

10   A small, passionate team can accomplish more than a crowd.

Teamwork and cooperation are inspiring, no matter what the situation. I worked for a health and fitness nonprofit, a running organization, that was the organizer of the world's largest 10K road race. Each year on July 4, sixty thousand participants take to the streets and run the Peachtree Road Race. I worked in brand marketing for the organization, which at the time was based in a small house with fewer than twenty full-time staff members. My first year working the race, I was in disbelief that such a small team could rally volunteers and maximize resources in such a big way. I was overwhelmed with emotion as I moved through a sea of people celebrating their race finishes, and in that moment, I learned that passion matters more than size and to never underestimate or overlook a small team.

11 Don't go into a situation saying, "I can't do this," or, "It can't be done." Go in saying, "How can we get this done?"

12 You'll do your best work when you are mildly uncomfortable.

This was a mantra of a former boss of mine. He shared this with me and my colleagues on his very first day on the job, and he held us to it throughout our time together. He could often be found pushing us outside of our comfort zones, expecting more, or conditioning us to expect more of ourselves. At the time I first heard the phrase, I remember questioning it, thinking *I likely do my best work when I'm comfortable.* But I know now that he was right; I did some of my very best work in that job. You'll do your best work when you feel confident enough to try, but vulnerable enough to work your absolute hardest to make sure you don't fail.

13   Gossiping won't solve the problem. I promise.

Does a lack of communication cause the whispering or does the whispering cause a lack of communication? No matter where you work, there will always be office gossip and people whispering or messaging behind each other's backs. A gossip-filled environment tends to go hand-in-hand with a lack of communication in the workplace. It's a "chicken or the egg" situation, and I haven't figured out which comes first, but I know one thing for sure: Gossiping won't solve the problem, so just don't do it. Instead, institute methods of clear and constant communication where you can; a weekly status meeting, a daily fifteen-minute check-in, a board for questions and answers. And don't be afraid to seek the truth from superiors or teammates, it's always helpful and respected to go to the source.

14   Support and motivate women in business, especially if you are another woman.

I worked for a male-dominated athletic company, but had a fearless woman boss. In what felt and seemed like a regular meeting, we once found ourselves at a conference table filled only with other women. I and many of my colleagues were all too busy to notice, but my boss took a moment to recognize each woman and her accomplishments. She went around the table highlighting a strength in each person and bringing to our attention the ways we all work together to get stuff done. She also pointed out to us that there were no men sitting with us, which was rare at this company. This moment was a great reminder that women should always support each other and not compete for what are still often too few seats available at the table.

15 Only make the great ones.

Having the opportunity to hear directly from a visionary leader and entrepreneur is a gift. I was fortunate to work for one of the world's largest athletic brands while the young and impressive founder was still the CEO and would address the entire global company at town hall meetings. In a time of crisis for the company, he discussed discipline and changes the company would be making, and this is one of the things he said: "We will only make the great ones." I loved this line. This was a challenging statement to some of the product teams at the company, which might make one product—a certain shoe, for example—and then simply vary it slightly in color or texture to make many. The CEO went on to say that we would no longer be using our resources to make fourteen different colorways of the same shoe. That there was no way they were all great, and the company should be more critical and only produce the great ones. This was a valuable lesson in business for me. By making more variety of the same, what if all you've done is dilute the product and its greatness by providing too many options? Conserve your financial and energetic resources, and don't waste time producing average work or average products just to make more.

16   Spend at least one day in your life working on your feet all day.

Standing on your feet and talking to people all day is one of the best ways to be a true ambassador for your company and to hear directly from those you are selling to or working with. The most common examples that come to mind are working a retail job or in food service as a waiter or host. I somehow missed those rites of passage, having worked in a photography studio as my high school and college job, but later in life I represented a brand I worked for at the Consumer Electronics Show, commonly referred to as CES, in Las Vegas. It's an out-of-this-world tradeshow for tech and innovation that attracts close to two hundred thousand attendees over four days. I was on the show floor talking to potential partners and clients and demonstrating products for ten-plus hours every day, and it was equal parts exhausting and exhilarating. If you've never been in a career where your job required this of you, consider recruiting or promoting for your company at an event or working in your brand's retail store for a day so you can understand the contribution.

17   Make career decisions based on what's right for you, not what's right for other people.

The people you work with are important. I've encountered big decisions about leaving a job or taking on a new role, and typically the first thing that comes to mind is the people. Either being sad about the ones you are leaving behind or curious about the ones you will be joining. It can be hard to separate yourself from others when it comes to decisions about your role, because they can be so intertwined, but it must be done. Things are often in motion that we are completely unaware of, decisions about promotions, departures, reorganizations. On any given day, your boss could leave the company or a coworker could be let go and then you might find yourself wishing you'd done something differently. When deciding whether to stay in a role or take a new one, make the best decision for your current and future self, independent of other people.

18 Give your best, even when things are the worst.

To some degree, the level of visibility of a project makes it possible to endure hardship behind the scenes. Maybe it's work people have heard of, or maybe the reward is great in the end. But there is also work for unknown brands—or well-known brands with clients who make life difficult—with no great reward at the end. I know this to be true from both sides of the work, being the client and working for one. My brother has worked on some very well-known brands in his time as a graphic designer and as a creative director too. We were once discussing a project and a client that he was having a particularly hard time with. I could tell he was checked-out and not giving it his all. I was trying to empathize while also doing my job of motivating him to be better. My brother and I are very into sports, and the sports analogy I used on him that day is a great reminder of how you should show up for your work and those you work with: "You can't only give your best when your team is winning. You have to give your best when you're on the worst team in the league and down 0–5 for the eleventh game in a row." You can't only give your best when it's the best client or your favorite project. You should always take pride in your work, you never know who could see it or what good might come from it. Give your best to the worst stuff too.

19   Never answer a hypothetical question from a reporter.

This was applicable to my work life, but it's a good piece of advice for anyone's general adult life too. Saying something "off the record" can be tricky ground. When reporters ask hypothetical questions, they are often recording verbatim what you say even if the question is only hypothetical, which can then be used out of context in an article or clip later. Be careful what you say, as you might read or hear about it later.

20   Losses make for better, more intentional future wins.

Losing a pitch, competition, job, anything really, can be heartbreaking. I played sports all my life and was fortunate to be on a lot of winning teams, but I lost plenty of times too. In my career I've lost agency pitches, campaign ideas, coworkers I've cared about, and even a job once. I've learned a lot from losing, primarily that losing offers you an opportunity to identify and evaluate why you lost and to train and fine-tune your approach so that you don't lose again.

21 Your cover letter simply needs to get you an interview, not the job.

I've written more than a hundred cover letters in my time. From all of my experience in this area has emerged one very important realization: Your cover letter doesn't need to get you the job, only the interview. You don't have to include all of your experience or your entire life story, so please keep it under the one-page limit. You just need to be interesting and qualified enough to get the interview, and then you can tell them more once you've gained the first step.

22 Don't be too busy to be great.

It's easy to get busy in your work. But don't be so busy becoming "great" that you forget to actually *be* great—great in what you do, great in the way you communicate, great in the way you treat others. I was working in brand management for one of the world's largest athletic brands and all day, every day was a hustle, but I felt accomplished from the high visibility and the level of work we were doing.

In this specific case, I was doing some product testing and interviews with consumers on a tight budget. I was doing all the parts: the recruiting, the communicating, the interviewing, the recording, and the incentivizing, and I loved it all. But this was in addition to all of the other regular daily marketing work and tasks I had on my plate. I can remember heading into a consumer interview late at the end of one day. I recall that other people were leaving campus when I was walking into this meeting room. As I set up my makeshift camera for the interview and got to know the participant, I realized I had forgotten to communicate something and also realized I had forgotten to bring along the gift card to be given as a thank-you for participating.

Here I had felt proud just to have coordinated this interview, arrived on time, and gotten my camera set up, but the lack of proper communication and the lack of preparedness was not like me, and I felt it. Thankfully the participant was understanding and I was able to make things right by email later, but there was a moment when I stopped and internally questioned myself, *Are you being too busy to be great?* And so that evening as I returned to my desk, where I was often joined by the office cleaning crew, I pledged to myself to not let the pace of my work change the quality of my care for it.

23 Before an interview, file your nails, wear comfortable clothes, and don't try anything new with your hair.

24 Always answer your work phone enthusiastically.

You never know who will be on the other end. I once received a call on my work line from another agency that was interested in having me come interview for a position. I initially found it bizarre and uncomfortable that they called me at work, when an email or LinkedIn message would have sufficed. But I later realized it was a first test; they got to hear how I presented myself and were able to see how I'd navigate a slightly uncomfortable situation at work. It can be easy to let the fatigue of phone calls get you down and damper your enthusiasm, but simply don't be drab when you answer your phone—you have no way of knowing what might await you on the other side of the next ring.

25 No matter your role, share your point of view; you are the only one who has it.

It's been mentioned already in this book that I've been fortunate to be in jobs where I found myself seated at tables with giants, amazing veterans of industry, whom I've felt grateful to be next to, but also sometimes intimidated by. It was vital to my career and I believe it will be vital to yours, too, that you understand that no one knows exactly what you know or sees things exactly as you see them. Sure, maybe someone has a similar background. Maybe they worked for the same previous employer, but you likely weren't there at the same time or in the exact same role. And even if by some chance they were, they don't have your personal experience or your perspective. You are the only you, so share your point of view.

I interned on an automotive account in the summer of 2009, during a very specific season when the government had initiated a rebate program for car-buying to boost the economy. I worked for several fast-food clients right at the time that the FDA first required calorie counts on menus and advertising, changing the way we worked and visually communicated. I started working at the second largest road-running organization in the country on the very day of the Boston Marathon bombings in 2013. This isn't a chronological inventory of my work history, but just a few examples of instances and occurrences that make my experience unlike any others'. No one has seen what I've seen in the way that I've seen it, and the same is true for you.

Prompt: What experiences have you had, personal or professional, that make your point of view unique?

_____

_____

_____

_____

_____

_____

26 Work to appreciate the times you don't have to.

It's safe to assume I wrote this on a Tuesday after a three-day holiday weekend, one of those days where you're still riding the high from being with friends and family and sleeping in. Remember that work is necessary and important, and that we understand and appreciate days off because we know what days on feel like.

Prompt: What do you do on days off that makes your life more meaningful? How can you incorporate these activities into your days on?

_____

_____

_____

_____

_____

_____

_____

27   If you're going to study for a big test or start a business, you need a comfortable chair.

If you're committing to something big, commit to providing yourself with what you need to be successful. I made a big life shift and decided I was going to both study for the GRE (a standardized test used in graduate school admissions) and start doing freelance work. I technically had a home office and a desk, but I never used them because I had no chair to sit in. Working at the dining room table was proving to be both counterproductive and uncomfortable, so I made an investment and bought a good chair for the desk, in part because it was more comfortable, but also because it was an outward sign that I was committed to my new plan.

Prompt: What ways can you show yourself and others that you are committed to your plans for growth?

_____

_____

_____

_____

_____

28 Don't start a business email with "My apologies for . . ." You immediately diminish your authority by opening with an apology.

"My apologies for the delay," "I'm sorry I wasn't able to get back to you yesterday," these are very possible and probable things you might include in an email to a client, vendor, etc. In my first job as an account coordinator at an advertising agency, I too started an email to a client with an apology and I'll never forget it. I was fortunate to work on more than one account under multiple leaders, and this particular client lead walked over to my desk after I sent the email and shared this piece of advice: "Never start an email with *my apologies for.*" He went on to tell me how he believes that such a statement immediately diminishes your authority and position, and that there are other ways to express your sentiment or share your update. This very small piece of advice has stuck with me for quite some time.

At times I'll be writing an email and still find myself thinking an apology internally, but instead I write, "Dear Client, Thank you for your patience in my reply . . . " Being grateful feels and appears much better than being sorry. As a young employee, it also meant a great deal to me that this senior leader walked over to my desk to impart this piece of wisdom.

Prompt: Who has been an important boss or mentor in your career? What is something they did or said that you've committed to memory?

_____

_____

_____

_____

_____

_____

_____

_____

_____

_____

29   Part of being a professional is handling rejection maturely.

Rejection is inevitable in your career. Whether it's an idea, a body of work, a meeting proposal, or you as a whole being, at some point you are going to offer something that is rejected by a boss, by a client, by your team, or by a prospective employer. It's a fact you need to understand and expect so it doesn't set you back too much when it happens. I have a particular experience of rejection that stands out because it's not what you'd expect when you talk about rejection. It didn't come from being turned down for a position I applied for or being told that an idea I presented wouldn't work.

It came from a client who told me I was doing a good job. I had been promoted after my first year of work from coordinator to manager, and in addition to the large account I worked on with a team, I now managed my own small piece of business for my agency. As this was me stepping out on my own, I was creating new systems and overcommunicating in the hope of making a great impression. In a meeting the client said that I was doing a "good job, but not a great job." They went out of their way to overemphasize "good" in a way to make it seem simply average or satisfactory. They followed this statement with what they'd like to see done differently and shared other systems that would work better for them than what I had created. This feedback caught me off guard, as I'd been working so hard to impress them that their disapproval hurt even more. But I used this rejection as motivation to work even harder and get to know them and their ways of working better. I knew then that I never wanted to hear someone say that I was doing a good job again; I wanted my work to only be described as great or excellent.

Prompt: Think of the last time you or one of your ideas were rejected. How did you feel and how can you use the rejection to improve?

_____

_____

_____

_____

_____

_____

_____

_____

_____

30   Find the sweet spot where your talents and values meet. Work there and stay there.

I knew a few of my talents when I started working: I was observant at noticing things that others didn't, I had a unique skill for filtering succinct themes from lengthy stories or multiple bodies of work, and I was particularly adept at communicating and at managing relationships. I searched for roles where I could not only put these traits to good use, but also continue to fine-tune them. I didn't know a lot about values when I first started working, or at least not values in regards to work or alignment with my personal brand and beliefs. I only knew about values as they pertained to morals or family values—but values are important to your work life too. Your personal values are your gut check and rallying cry, the things that you can use as guideposts to understand what's right and not right for you, where you should engage and contribute your talents, in life and in business. It's important to know these so you can make decisions about organizations, partnerships, and associations as you grow your career. Find your sweet spot, that perfect intersection where the talents you've nurtured and the values you've developed meet.

Prompt: Fill in your talents and your values, defined as your personal priorities or your guideposts for what you believe is right and good, below:

Talents   Values

_____   _____

_____   _____

_____   _____

Write down a potential organization or role where your talents and values could meet:

_____

_____

31 Meet the people you will actually be working with before you commit to working with them.

Gone are the days of arranged marriages for most cultures, so why should arranged employment be any different? Statistics show we'll spend a third of our lives working, and since we spend more time at work than we do at home each day, we should choose these people with the same care we would exert in choosing a life partner.

I once accepted a job without having met anyone except the CEO of the organization. In hindsight, I truly cannot believe I did this. While I was taking on a position where I would be working with the CEO directly, there were many other people I'd be working with too, and I should have met at least one of them. It was a big mistake and it showed right away. Over the course of a few weeks it became clear that I wasn't the best fit for this role or this organizational culture, but even on my first day, I had not a single existing conversation or connection to rely on. I can't be sure that having met others would have allowed me to see the mismatch that this role was for me, but I can be sure that it would have been nice to at least have met someone else prior to my very first day.

Meet the people you'll be working with. It gives you a more intimate understanding of the culture, a glimpse into the future goals and past experience of your peers, an opportunity to ask about the leadership, and if nothing else, maybe someone to grab lunch with on your first day.

Prompt: What characteristics are most important to you in coworkers? In a company culture?

_____

_____

_____

_____

_____

What would be a red flag that a company or team wouldn't be the right fit for you?

_____

_____

_____

_____

_____

32 Don't pretend to be someone you are not at an interview.

Be the most you that you can be at an interview. When I interviewed for what became the second role in my career, a brand marketing job at a health and fitness nonprofit, I felt so much like myself. I was confident, at ease in the company of my future boss, candid about my big ideas for the company, and easily able to relate my personal passion and professional experience to the role. I left the interview knowing that I had been natural and that if I got the job it was because they genuinely liked me and my ideas. It wasn't until I had this experience that I realized I had previously been in interviews where I was pretending. Pretending to know more than I did about media or pretending to be more interested in a client than I was. You shouldn't pretend to be someone you are not, because you don't want to have to pretend every day for the rest of your time at that company. Conversely, if you leave an interview feeling like you were able to truly be yourself, then there's real value in that and you should work diligently to secure that job.

Prompt: How do you know what "being yourself" feels like? What does it mean to "be you"?

---

33   Always be prepared with a five-minute version of your sixty-minute presentation.

Scheduling changes happen. Other meetings run late. C-level team members are often double-booked or only partially present for meetings. Don't be caught off guard when this happens to you; be prepared with a shortened version of whatever it is you are working on. A quick refresher on the problem or opportunity combined with your recommendation—the elevator pitch, if you will. It's possible you could prepare an entire sixty-minute presentation and only end up getting five minutes to speak. Make the most of it.

Prompt: Think of a time when you had to be spontaneous at work. What did that experience teach you?

_____

_____

_____

_____

_____

_____

34   The way you feel about your manager is likely the way they feel about theirs.

Management style has a way of trickling down through an organization. Information and the style in which it's communicated is often a product of the environment. I worked for a company with lean staff resources and way too many meetings, so on many days I would have double- and triple-booked times on my calendar. My boss was often hurried, showing up late to meetings or leaving early, sometimes asking me to represent her in meetings that I wasn't necessarily equipped with the information to be in. I got by in those meetings, and I always did the best I could with the information I had. As my exposure to the company and higher levels within it increased, I realized that my boss was doing the same, getting by and doing the best she could with the information she had. So, look around and above you. If your manager is often hurried, short, or providing incomplete information, it's possible that is the message or notion being passed on to them from their manager. Break the chain for those that you manage. Be the type of manager you would like to have.

Prompt: What have the people you manage or who are less senior shown you or taught you? What do you think you've shown them?

_____

_____

_____

_____

_____

_____

_____

_____

35 Leading and doing are not mutually exclusive.

A boss once told me I was a "doer" and not a leader. That comment felt terribly insulting to me at first, as I have always considered myself a leader. But I admit it's true. I can be a control freak at times, and I'm definitely a "doer" too, someone who can roll up her sleeves and get the work done. As you lead in life, make sure your teammates know you're right there doing with them, willing to get messy and work hard for the greater good. And as you are doing, it's very possible you are leading, too. Leading in the innovation of what you are doing, or in a particularly creative or diligent way that you are doing something. As you do in life, notice the opportunities that you have to lead, to show others the way simply through the example of your hard and smart work. Leading and doing go together.

Prompt: In what area of your life do you have the strength and skills to both lead and work?

_____

_____

_____

_____

_____

36   Ask yourself, "What do I do for fun?" and consider how you could make that your life's work.

The idea of work comes from being so talented at something that someone else asks you to do it for them. And I'm not talking about opening tough jars or getting knots out of jewelry. I believe your work should allow you to contribute to your network and to society with one thing that you enjoy doing for others. That last part is key. Not only should you be great at your work, but you should truly enjoy doing it, whether by way of being challenged by it and enjoying solving the problems it presents or simply by having pure fun when you do it. Take inventory of the things you like doing for fun—maybe it's listening to friends and helping with their problems and you should consider being a counselor. Or maybe you love numbers and creating budgets and you should consider a transition to something in finance. Or maybe it's taking things apart and putting them back together and you could become an electrician or mechanic. Whatever they might be, take note of these interests and dig more deeply into ways you could do them for work.

Prompt: So what is your thing (skill, talent, expertise)? And how can you make it your work?

_____

_____

_____

_____

37 If you haven't made the "30 Under 30" list, make your own list.

I've been fortunate to have talented friends and colleagues who were featured on the *Forbes* "30 Under 30" lists and others like it. I was always proud of them for this accomplishment and also always hard on myself for not making this kind of list. It had been a goal of mine to be a leader of industry who received this type of recognition. I'm now over thirty, and I can proudly say that I never made one of those lists, but I did check myself and this expectation I'd set, and instead I made a list of the thirty accomplishments in my life that I was most proud of. Take some time for yourself and do the same.

Prompt: Start your list. Write down at least ten things you are proud to have accomplished before thirty (or thirtyish).

_____

_____

_____

_____

_____

_____

_____

5 RELATIONSHIPS

Create a relationship that matters long before it matters.

Relationships often create opportunity where there is none. I got an interview for what became my first job because I visited that agency on a college trip and met a woman in recruiting and stayed in touch. I went back to meet with her again for an informational interview even though the company wasn't hiring, to express my continued interest and get to know her and the agency more. When they later won new business and were hiring, she called me and asked me if I'd be interested in applying for the position. I had cultivated a relationship that proved fruitful. Of course, I hoped this relationship would matter; I started it with that goal.

In my first working years, I further learned to create relationships that mattered, no matter what. I worked in one of the bigger buildings in downtown Atlanta, which had a large security desk in the center, right when you walked in. One member of the security team was very friendly, always expressing genuine interest in my day and my work, and I got to know a little bit about him and his family, too. He shared pieces of advice and inspiring stories from time to time, but thankfully he never took up too much time when I was running in or out. We were on a first-name basis, and a security guard is a good friend to make in a downtown urban landscape. I didn't know it then, but one day my credit card would be stolen while I was in the building's gym and I knew right who to go to. I also once got a flat tire in the building's parking garage, and he checked in on me as I waited for AAA to arrive. We had a relationship well before I needed help and it made it easier to call on him when I did.

You can enter these years in your twenties so self-focused, thinking things in regards to your relationships like, *What's in it for me?* or *Who are the right friends to make to get to the top?* But those are the wrong questions. It's important to note that you have no way of knowing right now which relationships might matter most later. Not all relationships reveal themselves to be beneficial, but any of them has the potential to become one of your greatest assets in life. Our days are made up of interactions, conversations, and connections that take place with other humans—and sometimes even with things—and this chapter is about all of that. No matter who you are and where you are, these lessons are applicable to how you engage (or don't) with the people who surround you.

It's important that you create a relationship that matters with someone long before it matters whether or not you have a relationship with that person. It can be so simple. Remember to say hello to the security guard every morning.

Be friendly to your IT teammate all the time, not just when you are submitting a repair ticket. Smile and speak to the neighbor you see in the elevator every day. Initiate and invest in the possibilities of relationships all around you, *just because*, and not because you'll gain from it. In the end, you most likely still will.

1   Surround yourself with people who are willing to lift as they climb.

You know these people. They are taking night classes, music lessons, or starting a business on the side while giving 100 percent to their full-time job. They are a professional athlete who does more reps right after the game or meet. The type of person who is always working to improve themselves or others for the future, while still giving everything they have to the present.

I've been fortunate to work and compete alongside people like this, and I'm better for it and grateful for it. There is one coworker in particular who inspired this lesson. I met him at my first job in Baltimore, Maryland. Upon one of our first encounters he asked me, "What is your side hustle?" He then went on to share that he believed everyone should have a passion they are working on that they enjoy outside of work. This particular person had more than one; he was writing a book and hosting a podcast, on top of working his full-time job at our company, a national nonprofit. He was doing a lot of heavy lifting. But he also inspired me with the time he took not only to improve his skills and prepare for alternate futures, but to motivate others to do the same along the way. In some way he was not only climbing and lifting his own weight, but giving others a lift too.

You want to work, live, and surround yourself with people who have this kind of drive and care for others. It's contagious.

2   Be the person you want to be talking to.

Do you know how good it feels to be heard and understood? I love it when I'm talking to someone and they convey a physical and emotional posture of interest. They get comfortable, open up, and act truly engaged and concerned with what I have to say. This is the kind of person I want to be talking to. And sometimes in a one-on-one conversation when I find myself thinking distracting thoughts, or if I'm in a group setting and feel myself and my ears veering to another conversation, I remind myself, *come back, stay engaged, show this person they are important.* I remember to be the person I want to be talking to.

Think of someone who always makes you feel seen, who is an excellent listener and contributor to your life. Emulate them when you are listening to others. It's great to feel heard and understood, and it's also great to make other people feel this way too.

3   Don't mistake someone who talks a lot for an expert.

4   Your best relationships will be the ones in which you understand each other, not necessarily agree with each other.

When I first moved in with my college roommate, my family could not understand how we could possibly get along or live together. She was a dancer; she loved pink, bedazzled jean jackets, and her room was leopard-print. I was none of those things. Based on visible interests alone, we might not look like perfectly suited best friends. But we are. We have a matching emotional intelligence, great listening skills, a respect for each other's choices, and thankfully, we do share an appreciation for a well-crafted dirty martini and fries, to start. The point is that you don't have to have everything in common to have a great relationship, whether it be as a friend, a coworker or a partner. You just need to understand where the other person is coming from.

5 Let people finish their sentences.

6 The people make the place.

It's easy to just overlook this as a common phrase. "The people make the place." Yes, I've heard it many times, but I've now experienced it many times, too. The first example that comes to mind is a time I returned as an old alumna to a college bar/restaurant that I'd often frequented with my girl-friends our senior year in college. It was one of those hole-in-the-wall places with unbelievably affordable pitchers of beer. I went back without all of the people that I had usually been there with. I was with just one friend, and instead of sitting for hours and ordering many pitchers, we found ourselves trying to hurry up to just finish our pitcher and leave.

I remember thinking, *who are all of these people and what have they done to this place?* But nothing about the physical place had really changed, only the people in it, and the fact that I now didn't know any of them.

I've also had experiences where I've been shown a new place through the eyes of another, and thus the memories of that place are connected to that person. Appreciate the people who contribute to your surroundings. The place you are in, whether it be a physical space or a mental state, wouldn't be the same without them in it.

7 Be on the lookout for "direction by affection."

I learned this one from our dog. Dogs lick or nudge in order to get what they want from you, whether it's food in their bowl or a back scratch. We humans are often guilty of using affection in the exact same way, asking for a favor through actions like a kiss on the cheek or a gentle hand on the back. That's not necessarily a bad thing, but be aware of how you use affection and if some people in your life are only affectionate, physically or verbally, when they want you to do a favor for them. Don't ever use affection on others only as a guiding direction, and don't let it happen to you. Be sure that sometimes affection is simply just that.

8 Every time someone is speaking, it's an opportunity for you to be learning.

Lean in, listen, and learn. One year in my late twenties, my husband and I went on vacation to Tucson, Arizona to escape winter. We stayed at a beautiful ranch hotel, and one afternoon there was a hotel happy hour where many guests were mingling. We struck up a conversation with another guest about some of the hiking we'd done. He turned out to be a serious and more extreme hiker, and we learned some great tips for the trails we had planned for the next day. The man's wife joined our conversation and she elegantly transitioned the conversation to what we did for work. I, at the time, worked for a large athletic brand and my husband for a large consulting firm. She found both of our roles interesting, was able to relate to our work, and then revealed that she was a thirty-plus-year vet of one of the largest and most well-known international management consulting firms. As we discussed work she went on to share that she was an author (a best-selling one, it turned out) and expert on women in the workplace. I had the opportunity to follow up with her on LinkedIn, and she also has graciously shared tips and support for my book-writing journey.

That day she was a stranger. She still is, though we've met once and exchanged messages once or twice more, but I had much to learn from her. You don't know who someone is or who they know or what might change in your life that you could learn about today. So when you can, take the time to meet and listen to others. There's always an opportunity to be learning, and you just never know who you might meet.

9   **Live and act so that people feel compelled by you, never coerced.**

10   **Don't let your confidence become conceit.**

An ego is not a bad thing. It's important to have a good self-esteem, to value your own self-worth. It's when your ego gets too large that things can become troublesome, when it's been boosted many times and you allow that inflation to show. It's okay to have an ego, just don't let it show.

11   **If you stay quiet, you give people the opportunity to wonder what you're thinking.**

I've been known to talk a lot. My mom tells stories of how much I talked as a toddler. My family may have called me "mouth of the South" growing up, and my husband has thankfully learned how to keep up with the frequency and cadence of my speech. Trust me, he's never really had to wonder what I'm thinking. But I've also learned the important skill and posture of listening. I've come to be known as a great listener and counselor among friends, family, and coworkers. I know how to lean in and listen, but also how to sit back and wait.

I was once in a meeting and hadn't expressed my thoughts on the topic at hand, when my boss said, "Michelle, what do you think?" and I realized then how powerful it can be to stay quiet. My opinion was asked for and now had center stage. I'm still very much a proponent of speaking up; I don't believe that you should always wait to be asked. But do practice the art of switching it up sometimes. Not only is letting others speak a gesture of respect, but if people have gotten used to hearing you jump in or insert your opinion, the change of pace might be intriguing to them.

12 Sharing isn't bragging.

Jobs, moves, engagements, promotions, weddings, inventions, babies, recoveries, and discoveries. There are a lot of things that might happen to you in early adulthood that deserve celebration. At times, it can feel selfish or hard to celebrate if you have friends working toward the same goal, but who are not quite there yet. I've been hesitant to share big milestones like a promotion or a proposal because of others' feelings, or for fear it would seem like I was bragging. But I shouldn't have been so self-conscious. I've realized that sharing your own happiness can bring other people happiness too. Don't feel conflicted or guilty about sharing your good news. The people who love you will want to celebrate you and your successes.

13 Take care of each other. We're all in this together.

I've been through the wringer seeing others achieve success before me, thinking I was in competition with my peers. I realized that in my early adulthood I was moving my own marker for success based on the achievements of others. But I've learned not only to focus on my own goals, but also that there's space for everyone. Even if you are in competition with someone, going after the same work or maybe even the same partner, there's no sense in tearing each other down. Bringing someone down doesn't lift you up any higher. In fact, it's actually really fun to have people around you while you are doing life. Keeping you sharp, looking out for you, and making you better. So remember to take good care of each other, even those you think might be against you and not for you; we need each other to keep doing all it is that we're doing.

14 There are four important intangible gifts you can give to someone: your time, your attention, your love, or a shared life experience.

15 Figure out what you'll do with the answer before you ask the question.

Have you ever wondered why we ask questions? If the answer doesn't affect our actions or beliefs, then why do we even ask? Here I am asking confusing questions about questions. To get to the point, I once asked a significant other an important question about someone he had previously dated.

But before I asked him this out loud, I had to ask myself how the two possible answers he might give influenced what I would do next. I knew ahead of time why I was asking the question; it would help to reveal the sincerity of our current relationship and how serious it was or was not. And I had a response of my own in mind, based on his reply. It would have been emotionally dangerous and unproductive to ask the question and shrug off the answer. When you are asking big questions, be prepared to act on the answers.

16   Be a good gift giver and a gracious receiver.

17   We don't know what good deeds our good deed might inspire.

My uncle passed away at an unexpectedly early age due to a very quick and severe cancer. He was a particularly funny guy, always telling really good and sometimes really corny jokes. On the one-year anniversary of his passing I wanted to send my mom some flowers with a joke in the message to brighten her day. I reached out to another uncle to seek inspiration for a good joke. He loved the idea and happily contributed some thoughts. What I later learned is that my idea to send my mom flowers inspired my uncle to also send flowers to my late uncle's wife.

You could drop a twenty-dollar bill in a street musician's

jar and not know that they donate half of it to a nonprofit. Or you might buy a coffee for the person in line behind you and not know that they then feel inspired to buy coffees for the next two people. We don't often get to see what good deeds our own good deeds might inspire or create, but when we do it feels like such a gift.

18   Be more like the other person for the other person.

This is true of romantic relationships, but also of friendships and professional relationships too. Sometimes, you'll need someone to be more like you for yourself, and sometimes you'll need to be more like them for them. My husband reacts really enthusiastically any time I share big news, and so when he shares big news I now react that way for him too. I can't pick him up and spin him around in a circle, but we hug and spin instead. My mom goes out of her way to make birthdays super special, so I now do the same for her. I love handwritten notes and to send snail mail, and thankfully friends have caught on and sent me notes back. People show us their preferences in the way that they treat and react to us, so it's not hard to do things that will make them feel good. It's about understanding what the other person needs, respecting how they would do it, and sometimes doing exactly that in return.

19   Say things in ways people don't expect and they'll remember them.

Make your message memorable by using uncommon language. Ask for "fresh linens" instead of "clean sheets," or call the "strange landscape" an "unusual terrain" and people will pay attention. Using words to express yourself that people don't hear or say as frequently will make it more likely they'll remember what you had to say or at least how you said it.

20   Ask about what is good or what is best.

Think about how often we ask one another, "How are you? What's new?" and the recipient of this question says something like, "Not much" or "Just busy with work." What if instead of asking, "What is new?" we asked, "What is good for you right now?" or "What in your life is at its best right now?" I believe that by changing a simple greeting and question we can learn more about each other and it will likely and more immediately become a deeper conversation.

21   Own your untidy.

It is okay to let people see the untidy version of your life, meaning both you and your home. Let others in, even when it's messy. As much as you might want to, you can't be both interesting and neat all the time.

22   Weigh your comments carefully if you want your comments to have weight.

23   Judging one's character can mean more than judging one's actions.

There is a difference between using nouns and using verbs, not just grammatically, but in terms of tone and effect on another person. For instance, calling someone a cheater is likely to make a greater, more lasting impact on them than to say they cheated. This happened to me once. I knew someone who would say, "No, I didn't call you a liar, I just said that you lied." And as annoying as this is because I know the essence is the same, I also understand that the ways these words come across can seem different. In another example, my husband recently said to me, "You lack vision," when he claims he only meant to say I struggled to visualize something. Let's just say I haven't forgotten that one. Praising or rebuking one's character might mean more than simply commenting on their actions.

24   Pause for laughter.

I enjoy public speaking, but I hate practicing any presentation or speech in front of others. There's something about the real dance that excites me, but I've never been good at the pretending part. There's no way to actually give your real speech or presentation because you don't have a genuine audience. I was scheduled to speak at my best friend's wedding, and my husband was concerned I had not practiced. With very little effort or enthusiasm, I practiced for him. He had never seen me speak in public before and he was concerned, to say the least. He made comments like "Is that how you're going to do it?" and "Don't you think you should practice a few more times?" and I told him I didn't want to. He gave me a little too much public speaking advice and I was offended. But in his defense, he'd never seen me give a speech. The one piece of advice that stuck with me was, "If people actually laugh at your jokes, don't forget to pause for laughter." I loved that, and, thankfully, I did a lot of pausing the next day as people laughed at my jokes. In a speech or presentation and in life, remember to pause for laughter. Let each moment have its time.

25 The only real trouble with the truth is once you have it, you are stuck with it and have to figure out what to do with it.

26 People desire or want only what they are capable of comprehending.

Don't let someone's current (and often limited) understanding hinder your ideas for innovation. Most human minds can only understand what they've seen or known. As Henry Ford said, "If I had asked people what they wanted, they would have said faster horses."

27   Power outages can bring people closer together.

In my experience, power outages often encourage you to move toward the biggest, most well-lit space, pending no other imminent danger. For some, that's the living room or common area instead of their bedroom; for others, it's outside their house. Either environment typically guides us toward interactions with other people. I grew up in Florida, and I've had my fair share of days without power during hurricane seasons, and these situations usually made for extra family time. We played more games of cards by candle-light and sometimes had unexpected conversations outside with neighbors as we'd discuss what happened or when we thought the power would come back on.

But I have one example of a story that brought me closer to someone emotionally. I was with a guy I was dating, we were watching a movie, and the power went out—and so, as I had been conditioned, I suggested we play cards by candlelight. As the game started, we started asking each other big questions too. We got into such a deep and meaningful conversation that when the power came back on hours later, we quickly turned the lights off so we could keep our mood and atmosphere exactly as they were, more intentional and thoughtful, as we talked quietly in the low light. While it might not be the most obvious bonding experience, unexpected darkness has a way of pushing you into the light physically and sometimes it can have that same effect on your emotions too.

28   Leave room for others to be great. Don't take up all of the space yourself.

This one can be hard during this phase of your life. In friendships or relationships where one or more parties are high achievers, be gracious. The second half of the decade of my twenties was filled with change. Change in location and multiple changes in jobs, and I was very fixated on my own professional success. The topic ruled conversations with my family members, friends, and my significant other. I know they cared about me, my moves, and my ultimate happiness, but I discovered that I had become very self-focused in the trials and changes that were happening to me. Particularly when it came to my significant other. Both of our careers are important, and yes, I had moved cities for his, but then I let my obsession with mine take over our time together. I was often only ever talking about work, recounting my day, priding myself on my accomplishments, lamenting things I wish I'd done differently, and ultimately always wondering and plotting aloud about what was next for me. In conversation, don't forget to ask about the other person's day or accomplishments. In life, take their career or opportunities into account when making plans or decisions. In short, don't fill all of the air and all of life with your own greatness; make room for the greatness of others.

Prompt: What are some ways you can support the greatness of others in your life? By providing time, space, advice?

_____

_____

_____

_____

_____

_____

29   Learn to accept, adjust to, and delight in your current reality and the people who exist in it.

It's so easy to do future living. To imagine who you'll be, who you'll be with, where you'll live and work. What's hard is to accept and settle into where you are. And to go even one step further and not only accept where you are, but delight in it. Take a moment to inventory whether you do this, or if you think you are capable of doing this. Take note of all the good going on and all the good in those who are sharing this life stage with you. It won't be like this forever, so take it in and find joy in it, even the parts you aren't quite satisfied with. Now is all for a reason, and it is only for the present.

Prompt: What is something in your present moment that you find joy in?

_____

_____

_____

_____

_____

_____

Prompt: Finding joy or expressing gratitude are good practices for being present. What other tactics or practices can you count on to make yourself more aware of the present moment when you are in the presence of others?

_____

_____

_____

_____

_____

_____

30   Nurture your network.

Even with the luxury of all the technology we have access to, staying in touch with friends or former colleagues in other cities can be difficult. Maintaining a relationship when you see each other in person more regularly is still often easier. But it's vital that you strengthen and nurture your network, no matter where you are. I was once on a walk with a former boss and told her I admired the ways that she had nurtured her network and regretted that I had not. She told me it was never too late, that I had access to many of the people in that same network, and that I should never hesitate to reach out. The worst thing that could happen is that someone won't respond or they'll say they are too busy to connect.

This is true of every relationship—don't hesitate to reach out. Maintain your friendships and connections even after you leave a job or move to a different city. Make it a point to check in on your long-distance friends every other week and share an update with your former work colleagues once a quarter. It's good for your professional life and the success of your work, but it's also good for your friendships and the quality of your life.

Prompt: Who do you want on your team, right now and in the future? Make a list of five friends and five former colleague relationships you intend to nurture. (Note: If you don't have former colleagues yet, identify current ones or past teachers, mentors, etc.) Set dates to connect with them by, and follow up on them.

_____

_____

_____

_____

_____

_____

_____

31 You may make plans for yourself, but don't forget that the other people in your life are making plans too.

Have you ever been dreaming of your favorite Italian restaurant when your date simultaneously suggests sushi? Or been planning on sleeping in when a friend suggests you wake up for a five a.m. workout class? I'll never forget the first time my family went on vacation as a new family of six, when my brother and I both brought significant others. I remember discussing with my now-husband that we'd wake up and go for a hike, but coming out to the living room to find my brother sleeping in, and my parents cooking a big breakfast and discussing plans for driving to the shops in town.

Family vacations, date nights, group activities . . . you can't help but form expectations about what you hope to do during these events. But remember, you're not going it alone. Recognize that in the same way you make plans and form expectations, others do too. Speaking up and learning to compromise are two of the most important skills you'll need to navigate the relationships in your life.

Prompt: How have you noticed your personality or actions change when you are in the company of others? Why do you think you make this change?

_____

_____

_____

_____

_____

_____

_____

_____

32   There's nothing like a beer at a baseball game.

While living in Atlanta, my brother and I went to many Atlanta Braves baseball games at Turner Field. Any time I'd make it to my seat with a beer in hand I'd think, *ahh, nothing like a beer and a baseball game.* This combination was just really enjoyable for me. It made me realize that combinations of activities can really make an experience. Popcorn and a movie. Summer and a cookout. A swimming pool and an umbrella drink. A walk and a spring day. Without one component the other wouldn't be quite as enjoyable and memorable. Take note of these things in your life, the combinations that have a way of making your day.

Prompt: What is a combination that really creates an experience for you? And what feelings does it combine?

_____

_____

_____

_____

_____

_____

33 What kind of people would we be if we only kept the company of those we agree with?

Seriously, how boring would this life be? I discovered this lesson while on the phone with my brother. I remember that I was driving home from work, but I can't remember exactly what we were talking about. Just that we were discussing something we didn't see eye-to-eye on, but that the conversation was such a good one. He helped me realize how important it is to disagree sometimes. Through respectful debate and discussion, we open ourselves up to another's perspective and gain a new way of looking at the world. This would never happen if we only filled our days with people who already agreed with us.

Prompt: Do you have acquaintances who disagree with you on social or life issues? What do you disagree on and what have you learned from listening to their perspective?

34 **You may regret the things you don't say as much as those you do say.**

My brother and sister-in-law leapfrogged my husband and me into marriage, meaning they got engaged after us and then married about two months before us. Despite the way many others would feel in that situation, I truly didn't have a problem with it. The only thing that was tricky was the timing of some of their wedding events and things I had to do for my planning. I had arranged to do my final dress fitting the same day as their wedding rehearsal and dinner, making the day slightly hectic for, of all people, my sweet mom. Early that morning, my mom was stressed, and my brother decided this was my fault. He was ironing his shirt for the day and said something to me like, "Was this really the only day you could do this?"—which it was, as I lived out of town and it was the only weekday I'd be in town again before my own wedding. So I replied to him by repeating the question, "Was this really the only day YOU could do this? I had this dress fitting planned first." Which implied that his wedding was in my way or that my activity was more important, neither of which were true to me. He said nothing in response, he just appeared hurt as he continued to now quietly iron his shirt. I immediately wished I'd just kept my mouth shut and that I hadn't tarnished his celebratory morning with my hurtful words.

That same night at the rehearsal dinner, we were all having a really wonderful and beautiful time. There was an open invite to stand up and speak, to share a few words. I had some great remarks to share and I was all set to speak. And then my brother's future father-in-law spoke and said the most meaningful things, specifically one thing about how our brother-sister relationship was a clear indication of my brother's level of nurture and care, leaving me blubbering at our table and unable to pull myself together and speak. I missed my window and then never found another one to stand up. I'm known to be the speaker of our family, and I didn't share anything at my own brother's wedding weekend.

And so you see, I've said hurtful things to people I've loved and I've also been too hurt, sad, or in this particular case, just too overwhelmed with emotion to speak up. I've regretted both situations. Recognize that regret doesn't only come for the words you've said, but also for the things you wish you'd said.

Prompt: Was there a time when you either said something you wish you hadn't or stayed quiet when you wish you had spoken up? What did you learn from this experience?

_____

_____

_____

_____

_____

_____

35   If someone you met in your last city visits you in your new city, that's a sign of enduring friendship.

I've lived in four different cities. As a self-proclaimed grand collector of professional experience, geographic adventure, and personal relationships, I know how valuable a relationship is that endures beyond location and convenience. It is one of the most precious gifts.

I have a close friend that I met in Atlanta. She was also a transplant to the city, originally from Toronto, and had moved there from Chicago. We worked for the same advertising agency, and I still remember her first day of work. She started just a month or two after I did. It was one of those situations where I immediately knew we were going to be good friends. Our cubicles were right next to each other; some days we ate breakfast, lunch, and dinner together, and we were the closest of friends. After a few years, we both went on to different jobs, but still saw each other for at least one happy hour and meal a week. I'll also never forget the last time we got together for drinks before I moved away from Atlanta. We both cried, almost hysterically, and continued to sob as we drove home separately. I know this because we came to a stop at the same red light and discovered each other crying behind the wheel—fortunately this brought us both a good laugh through our tears.

This friend was one of the first people to buy a ticket and come see me and my new city after I moved. It meant so much to me to know that our friendship, one that had only been formed five years before, could go the distance. When someone you met in your last city makes the effort to visit your new home and make it feel more familiar, appreciate it.

Prompt: Do you have a relationship that has endured a move or big life change? Describe what you appreciate most about that relationship.

_____

_____

_____

_____

_____

_____

_____

_____

_____

36 Living this life just for yourself is a waste.

Someone somewhere can benefit from what you've experienced and learned. I've been writing down all these things I've learned for years, thinking maybe one day I'd have a child and that he or she would be able to learn from my life. Or that some of the younger coworkers I've mentored would appreciate hearing about my discoveries and experiences. Sharing your stories and the experience you've gained, especially with those younger than you, allows your life to feel even more useful, and for some small part of you to be carried on.

Prompt: Who are you living this life for? What's the most important lesson you can share with them right now?

_____

_____

_____

_____

_____

_____

6 FAMILY

How we grow up influences what we see and look for.

My father is a carpenter, and he worked out of the attached garage at our home for much of my childhood. I grew up watching him work, building something new almost every day. Wood and stain were a regular part of my early life, and I can remember learning to "build" with some Elmer's wood glue and a few scrap pieces of wood he gave me. I can almost smell the scent of stain or paint just thinking about the days we couldn't go through the garage because my dad was spraying cabinets.

When I was growing up, I was very fortunate in that my dad handmade many things for me. He built a bookcase and a desk for me and even an innovative stand to hold my TV and maximize space in my dorm room when I went away to college. As an adult, I now love decorating my home with woodwork, and I don't think this is a coincidence. I've often joked that the home I share with my husband is a little reminiscent of a treehouse, as there are just so many fixtures and shades of wood to be found in it.

My father's work influenced more than just my preference

for cabinets; it also influenced my favorite colors, my appreciation for old things, and my expectations and standards for quality. Chances are you didn't have a carpenter for a dad, explaining how things were made or easily accessible out in the garage when you got home from school. Because our experience isn't the same, you and I might see the exact same thing very differently. How we grow up—what our families prioritize or don't, teach or don't, experienced or didn't—influences what we look for in the world and how we see and process things.

Family isn't just the people that we define as kin; it's the habits we form, the traditions we practice, and the ways we define ourselves as we set out on the journey of life. Even if you were missing a biological family as a child, that too influenced how you grew up and the way you see things now. Respect the differences that exist among "family" each time you encounter someone new, and consider that no one has the same family experience as you, except maybe your siblings.

This chapter is about the things I've learned from my own family and the friends I consider as such—lessons in appreciation, expectation, forgiveness, friendship, aging, and traditions and habits too. You might not be a sister, niece, cousin, aunt, mom, or daughter of a piano teacher and a carpenter, but I hope you can relate to the understanding that so much of who you've become or are yet to be is because of, and in spite of, your family, however you might define it.

1 It's nice to have a set of parents in town, even if they're not yours.

I moved to Atlanta one month after I graduated from college. I knew only two people in the city and met my roommate at my new job. She was from the area, and her parents lived nearby in a suburb of Atlanta. They would check on us from time to time, replenish our household products as a surprise, and take us to Sunday dinners. They weren't my parents, but they were loving parents, and I appreciated them for that. Even if you're independent and don't need your parents as much on a day-to-day basis anymore, you'll find that a little extra care, support, and a Costco-size pack of toilet paper are always helpful when you are living on your own.

2 Your siblings may be the most instrumental people in your life.

They know more about you than most other people, they are a built-in friend even if you don't believe you are the closest of friends, and they are the only people that have the same frame of reference, having most likely shared the same childhood as you. Never underestimate their role or impact.

3   When you have a second to call your mom, call her. You may not always have that chance.

Or your dad, aunt, or grandparent. Make time for the loved ones who are always there for you, who make you feel safe and comforted. When you have a chance to talk to that person, do it. There will come a time when that person is no longer alive to pick up.

4   Eat dinner at the table.

I don't mean all the time. Trust me, I know the couch is comfy, and I enjoy many dinners there. But when you are together with members of your family, try to eat dinner at the table. The position and focus of attention make for better conversation.

5   You should be the same you when you bring a significant other home as you are when you are visiting solo.

If this is happening, that's a good sign. I can remember being nervous that I'd act differently around my family when bringing home a new significant other that I'd met in Atlanta. My parents knew me well, but they were no longer with me on a day-to-day basis and my new significant other was. I wanted to make sure I was still myself; comfortable and at ease in our humble home, loving and potentially a little bossy to my parents, but respectful and allowing everyone to get to know each other. It's important to check in with both parties, your significant other and your family, and make sure they still think you seem like the "you" they know. You don't want to be with someone you can't be yourself around.

This goes for other family members too. You'll know your sibling has found a great significant other when they act the same around you as they always would. When my brother met his wife, he said, "I know she's the one because I'm myself with her. With her, I feel free and comfortable to act just like I do when I'm with you." Look for this as your siblings begin to seek a life partner, and keep them honest.

6 If you are fortunate enough to live in the same city as your siblings, see them often.

Being adults in the same city was a really great experience for my brother and me. We lived in Atlanta at the same time, overlapping there for three years. I was twenty-three and he was twenty-six when he moved there, and it was a transformative time for us, having both moved for new jobs and after ending long-term relationships. We saw each other for dinner once a week and went to a lot of good concerts together when we were both single. It's fun to reconnect as adults and get to know each other again, and it's one of the reasons my brother and I still have such a good relationship and friendship. We both met our lifetime partners there in Atlanta during that same time period, and it feels like an added bonus to have had the opportunity to see those relationships spark for each other.

I no longer live in the same city as my sibling, and I wish so badly that I did, that we could have weekly family dinners. But I now live in the same city as my brother-in-law, and I've passed on the importance of this lesson to my husband, encouraging him to see his brother often, whether it be for a workout or a dinner at our house. You don't know how long you'll live in the same city, and proximity is a luxury you don't always recognize and appreciate until it's gone.

7 Be less resistant to your parents' wants and needs.

I'm quick to do things my way and think that it is the best. Particularly with my parents, it's as though I think most of their ways are antiquated. An easy example that comes to mind is the way they ask for a printed receipt everywhere we go, so they can use it to balance their checkbook, when they could easily just check their balance online. But I'm learning to cede my way to theirs for the sake of enjoying our time together. There's no sense in arguing with them about how they don't need to do that, if they still enjoy the task of balancing a checkbook. Even if you don't always agree with your parents, their method, or what they want to do, try fighting against the impulse to advocate for what you think is best. Being agreeable will make your time together much sweeter.

8   If you ever have the chance to spend an extra $200 or drive an extra four hours to see your parents for even just one day, do it. It will be worth it!

In 2016, a huge snowstorm in the mid-Atlantic and Northeast left me stuck in Key West, Florida after a bachelorette party. The weather delay made it so that I was going to have to wait five extra days to get home to Maryland, and as great as five days in warm and sunny Key West sounds in the middle of winter, it wasn't going to be fun to be there by myself, and especially not after having already done a bachelorette party there for three days. When considering my options with the airline, I asked if it would be possible to fly out of Jacksonville, where my parents live, thinking that if I was going to be stranded in my home state, I wanted to be at home with them. I was able to get a flight out of Jacksonville much sooner than Key West, but since it wasn't my original flight location I had to pay a fee. It felt like a small price to pay to see my parents and have the comforts of home with the bonus of getting home to Maryland sooner too. So in one day I traversed the entire state of Florida, riding with a friend back to West Palm Beach and then renting my own car to drive an additional four hours to Jacksonville to spend time with my parents. But it was worth it all.

Yes, this is a very specific example in dollar amount and hours, but hopefully you get the point. When you get the chance to see your parents, even if it doesn't seem practical or convenient, do it.

9   Always make your mom's birthday a big deal. She made yours possible.

When my brother and I were growing up, my mom made our birthdays a really big deal. We had these summer birthday parties that our friends still talk about as adults, and the preparation for and anticipation of them were equally grand. We've often joked that our mother was the original Pinterest for children's birthday parties; she did research, checked out library books for certain themed parties, and hand-made wonderfully extravagant party details and favors.

As an adult, I try to make a big deal of my mom's birthday. Not only because she's always made a big deal of my birthday, but because she's the reason I even have a birthday. Now that I'm a mom myself, the biggest thing I've learned is that being a mother and birthing a child is indeed life-changing. So, make a big deal about your mom; celebrate her. If it weren't for her you wouldn't be reading this.

10   Everyone will encounter a time at a family event when it's best to just shut up and smile.

11 Pay attention when older family members are discussing their health.

I was at my aunt's house in South Carolina, sitting at the kitchen table with my mom and my aunt as they were discussing how they had both been diagnosed with high blood pressure and put on medication in their fifties. They went on to say that they weren't surprised because my grandmother had been as well, possibly even before she was fifty. This felt like a good time to listen up to see what else my fifty-year-old self might have to look forward to in the health department.

Not all medical and health issues are hereditary, but some of them are, so pay attention when your family members are talking about their health. It's good to be informed of the issues your family has and when they developed. In addition to allowing you to be there for your loved ones, it's also a free look into your potential future.

12 If you have the chance, spend time with each of your parents individually.

It might be clear that I have a really good relationship with my parents, that I actually want to see them and get sad when we go too long without seeing each other. I recognize that this is not the case for everyone, but I hope you can still relate to these thoughts in regard to some family member you are close with. I'm also already frightened for the day that I will no longer have my parents, and so it's important to me to see them, share as much as I can with them, and ultimately get to know them as the humans that they are, in addition to being my mom and dad.

You may view your parents as one unit, or maybe you never got to know one of them at all. Whatever your situation may be, once you've graduated childhood and moved into early adulthood, try to get to know your loved ones as individuals, to learn who they are, what they do now that you're gone, and what you might have inherited from each of them. The experience is different when you are just one-on-one.

13   Appreciate the airport at Thanksgiving.

I wouldn't be surprised if you have a questioning expression on your face after reading that line. People try hard to avoid the airport on the days surrounding Thanksgiving, and understandably so; it is, after all, the biggest travel holiday of the year. But there is also something special happening that is worth pointing out and admiring. I flew home to my parents in Florida for Thanksgiving for the first time when I was twenty-seven—every year prior to that I had lived somewhere from which I could drive home. So this was my first Thanksgiving airport experience and, yes, it was crowded and hectic. But I stopped for a moment as I realized that all of those people have other people they want to be with or are trying to get to. And I realized that even amongst the craziness, that is something to appreciate and feel good about.

14 Be your own family historian.

No two families are the same, but no matter who you are, it's important to know who and where you came from. One side of my family has an excellent family tree, a beautiful bound book of generations, names, births, marriages, deaths, and it is so interesting to look back and read about those that came before me. The other side of my family doesn't have this, or at least not nearly to the same extent, and I've tried to close the gaps where I can. I ask a lot of questions of my dad, and I've connected with my grandfather's sister, writing letters and gaining as much information about my grandparents and great-grandparents as I can. Ask lots of questions of your family members that are still living, travel to cities where your family has heritage, and write down what you've learned or experienced. It's never too late to start recording your family's history.

15 Tell your people how much you love them when you are overcome with it.

16 Get comfortable with a new pace.

Families grow and age and as they do, the pace at which they move changes. This happened first with my parents; as they approached sixty, they started to slow down a bit. They each had a surgery, one on a knee, the other on a back, and I began to notice that it took them longer to get moving in the morning. Or that we couldn't go quite as far on a hike as we once did, or definitely not as fast.

The next change in pace occurred when I became an aunt. As my immediate family expanded from a unit of four, then to six, to what was now a unit of seven, I noticed that when we were all together, we could no longer just get up and go. We had to account for all the schedules, including how long it would take my mom to get ready in the morning, and also when my new niece needed to be fed or take a nap. Without ever really discussing it, on our annual family cabin trips we started doing fewer activities outside of the house and spending more time playing cards or having drinks next to the fire.

Recognize that your parents might start to slow down. Instead of pushing their limits or encouraging them to keep up, keep them company and make them comfortable at their new pace. Accept that the pace of your family will continue to change, and as soon as you get the hang of it, it seems it changes again with age or new additions. Enjoy it, be together with the people, don't worry about the pace.

17 The truth will reveal itself.

My mom's parents divorced when she was six years old. Her dad, my grandfather, moved their family to Florida from their home in South Carolina and then left them there soon after. He had cheated on my grandmother and essentially started another family that he was returning to South Carolina to live with. It's safe to say my grandfather wasn't the best guy, but my mom says that she never heard her mom say one negative thing about him. Even after he cheated on her, uprooted her from her hometown, and left her. She rose above, never speaking badly of him and always allowing her children to visit their dad, his wife, and his new children.

As an adult, my uncle once asked my grandmother, "How did you never speak poorly of him to us or in front of us?" and she replied, "I didn't need to. I knew you'd figure it out on your own, that his true nature would reveal itself." Not only did she allow her children to form their own opinions, but she also maintained a posture of grace, never reducing herself by speaking poorly of her ex-husband.

18   Everyone's "normal" is different.

My family drove to Canada twice from Florida because my parents didn't like to fly. In fact, all of our family vacations were car trips. This was "normal" to me; I didn't know anything different. I didn't fly in an airplane until I was seventeen years old. As I grew up, I met people in college and beyond who had been flying in planes regularly since they were one month old; that was "normal" to them. Families are all different, and this is just one small example of how a lifestyle can be different from yours. As you age and encounter others in school, work, and beyond, remember that everyone's "normal" is different. Not just in travel and lifestyle preferences, but in the makeup of their family, their heritage, and their family customs and traditions too. As my Mom always says, "What's normal? Other than a setting on the dryer?"

19 Build more sandcastles.

Have you ever observed a family building a sandcastle at the beach? It's one of those precious moments where a family truly appears to be on vacation, enjoying a simple pleasure in life. When you are building a sandcastle, you are in it. Other times you are at the beach, but on your phone checking emails. Or at the beach, but going for a run, working on your fitness. When you are building a sandcastle, you are just there, committed to doing something slow, fun, and intentional with people you love. My husband taught me this lesson; we were once on the beach and he said, "I want to build more sandcastles." And I realized that he meant it literally, he wanted us to put down our books and build, but that he also meant he wanted us to prioritize the simple pleasures in life. To not be distracted or always achieving, to sometimes just slow down and enjoy the things that are before us. Especially those that remind us of being kids, so that one day we can practice doing them with our children too.

20 A mess might look different when it's yours.

I have a friend whose parents are divorced, and she has half- and step-siblings to keep track of on both sides. In addition to that, one of her stepsisters has several children of her own, making for a lot of limbs on her family tree and lots of guests at holidays. Any time this family got together, my friend wondered who and how many people would show up. It sounded hard to plan for. When I saw photos of their gatherings, sometimes it looked a bit messy. There were so many family members crammed together in a small house, and they all looked like members of different families, not the same one. But I once had the opportunity to hear from those directly in this family and all I heard about was the love they had for each other. I realized that I had been quick to judge from the outside, and that I actually had no idea what the inner workings of this family were like. To them it wasn't a mess at all.

21   Having two homes can make you more prepared.

This experience isn't firsthand, but I saw it growing up in a few of my close friends. One benefit of separated parents and having to live in two separate homes is that at a younger age you might be more mature and learn to be more prepared. Going to a different house midweek requires you to know when your science project is due and to take it with you. It also brings the maturity of anticipating and knowing what things you might need three days from now. I realize this isn't always the case, but some of my closest friends who grew up in two homes are also some of the most self-sufficient people I know.

22   Don't try to change your parents' habits. Appreciate them instead.

Things I know for a fact that I got from my parents: picking at my fingernails, putting other people's dishes and cups in the dishwasher before they are actually done with them, double-checking with whoever paid for dinner that they didn't forget their credit card. It's quite comical to watch me try to stop my mom from picking her nails when I later realize I'm doing it right next to her as we chat on the couch. Or when I comment, "Dad, please stop putting my cup away while I'm still using it," and later have to apologize to my husband for doing the same. It's silly that I think I'm "helping" them, making some kind of impact, or that I can change their habits at all. Stop trying to mess with your parents' habits, just let them be.

It feels important to note that when I think about my parents' habits, I realize it's not all bad or quirky stuff. More things I know for a fact that I got from my parents: giving more than one goodbye hug, knowing how to take good care of my things and make them last, feeling the need to provide for others, writing long handwritten thank-you notes. Next time you are with your parents, instead of trying to change their habits, try to appreciate their habits and take note of what you might have learned from them.

Prompt: What is a physical or emotional habit of yours that you inherited from your parents or a parental figure in your life?

_____

_____

_____

_____

_____

23 You are blessed if you are able to make new family holiday traditions while still having and taking part in your old ones.

Ask anyone who is married or in a serious relationship, and they'll tell you one of the hardest parts about growing up and growing together might be having to share or split up your holidays. Thanksgiving is my favorite holiday, and I still remember the first one I didn't spend with my family—and the first Christmas I wasn't home really didn't feel like Christmas to me either. But I've come to terms with this as I've realized how fortunate I am to now have more family and more traditions.

I came to this realization as I was decorating a Christmas tree with my husband in our home. It was our second year doing so, and we had made some traditions that we were carrying on from the previous year, such as where we purchased our tree, the music we listened to while we decorated, and even the order in which we put up some of the decorations.

We were decorating and "Winter Song" by Sara Bareilles came on our playlist. I felt myself tear up a little (it's a sentimental song), thinking about all the years I decorated a tree with my family of four and that my parents now had to decorate a tree by themselves. It occurred to me that instead of being sad, I should be overflowing with gratitude that I still have the opportunity to gather around a tree with those same people and now more. I wasn't being forced to make new traditions to fill a void from old ones that had been taken away, I was making new traditions on top of the ones I still get to participate in, though maybe now it's just every other year, or a few days after the holiday.

As your family expands, some of your traditions are bound to change, but the great news is, you get to make new ones.

Prompt: What is your favorite old and new holiday tradition? Are they related or very distinct?

_____

_____

_____

_____

_____

Prompt: What do these show you about your ability to adapt as your family and life have changed?

_____

_____

_____

_____

_____

24 Don't worry about your bedtime when you are with people you haven't seen in a long time.

I love to sleep! I wake up many mornings saying, *I just love sleeping and can't wait to go back to sleep tonight.* I'm sure many of you can relate to this feeling. But once in a while, it's important to prioritize time with family and friends over sleep. Don't worry about the amount of sleep you are getting; being together will energize you and more than make up for a few lost Zs.

Prompt: Who would you always stay up late for?

_____

_____

_____

_____

_____

_____

_____

25   **Make it better for the next generation.**

Both of my parents come from divorced families. It was important to them to show my brother and me something different than what they had. When they got married, they knew only a few people who had been married for longer than ten years. I am blessed to have many examples of long-lasting marriages in my life, but I'm particularly grateful for the role models that my parents are. For the ways they taught us about love, support, flexibility, and tolerance. For the vow they've kept to each other, but also the one that they made to us, to ensure that we saw something different and better than they did. As I write this, my parents have just celebrated their forty-second wedding anniversary. At this point I still can't even imagine being forty-two years old, much less spending that number of years with my husband. But I can't wait for it.

Prompt: What is a way that you are better off than your parents were? Is it because of something they did for you or something you did for yourself?

_____

_____

_____

_____

_____

7 MIND AND BODY

The most important nutrients are closest to the core.

Have you ever watched someone eat an apple? There are so many ways that people eat one: some take only a few bites before chucking it, some eat off all of the bites where the skin is still showing, and then there are those who eat all of the apple, all the way to the core. In those groups of apple eaters, I typically fall into the last one; I eat as much of an apple as I can without eating the seeds. I think the core tastes a little juicier and sweeter, and something about getting the most I can out of the apple feels particularly delicious and resourceful.

One night I was with my brother. We'd been drinking, and my twentysomething's apartment didn't have any good snacks in stock; I only had some healthy Fuji apples to offer. For some reason I can remember sitting on the ground with my legs crossed, enjoying my juicy apple. My brother laughed and remarked on the way I was eating my apple. He's more of the first, "only a few bites" camp of people. He said, "I can't believe you eat so much of the apple, do you eat the seeds?"

I grinned and just coyly said, "the most important nutrients are closest to the core."

I honestly made that line up, I didn't know exactly what I was saying when I said that aloud, but as I reflect on it, it's truly something I believe about myself and others. I think the most important things about me are the most intrinsic ones. The thoughts and beliefs that form in my mind, and the love that exists in my heart. But I also recognize that our exterior condition and the way we treat our physical bodies is vital to life here on earth. Plus, I've experienced many times how activities that happen to the body can affect the mind. Like how exercising boosts your mood and how sleep simply makes everything about our mental health better. The exterior and the interior are inextricably connected.

There are varying scientific opinions about which part of an apple is most nutritious. Some studies claim it is the skin, which delivers an abundance of vitamin K, while others claim that the core and seeds are packed with good-for-your-gut bacteria. The most obvious conclusion is that both the core (the mind) and the skin (the body) have benefits and deserve our attention and appreciation. This chapter covers a variety of learnings from my life that are in one way or another related to the mind and body, with lessons ranging from your fitness to your focus, and from drinking spirits to spiritual reflection. Some of what you will read might seem unconventional, but it's important that you learn that self-care should be self-defined. So take the time to figure out what works for you and determine what you believe.

1 Test in a small patch before applying.

This is wisdom handed down directly from rejuvenating facial mask manufacturers themselves. Those products very clearly state this on the directions: "Allergic reactions and skin irritations may occur. Before applying to the entire face, test in a small patch on the side of your neck or behind the ear." I couldn't agree more: Be careful what you apply to your face. This goes for everything; charcoal masks, sunscreens, lotions, serums, etc. Before applying anything to your face, try it elsewhere first—it's your one and only precious face, and it's hard to cover up. I once used a sunscreen I'd never used before while on a vacation with my friends, and I broke out in a rash all over my face. At first I thought the sunscreen hadn't worked and that I had been badly sunburnt, and instead I discovered that I was having some type of allergic reaction. Suddenly, a sunburn didn't sound that bad. I promise you, you don't want to go through having an unnecessary skin rash on your face when you have a weekend full of plans, or at any time really. And remember, this applies to all areas of your life too. Take on unknown things gradually and in small amounts, just a little patch at a time until you know it works for you.

2   Be careful at open bars. Just because you aren't paying for your drinks with money doesn't mean you won't pay for them.

Open bars—at weddings, corporate holiday parties, anywhere—are dangerous. It's so exciting to be at an open bar with your friends, especially when you are younger or on a budget, and someone else is paying for your good time. But that means you're likely to drink more because you're not pulling out your wallet and acknowledging the financial impact every time someone says, "another round?" I've been there more than once and it never ends well when you don't know how many drinks you had, trust me. I've been there at a wedding and the night ended with me throwing up in an empty shoebox in the guest room I was staying in, and then having to shamefully carry the shoebox out in front of others and hope that the owner of said shoebox didn't have plans to return her shoes. I've been there at a company holiday party and woken up the next morning with not only a terrible hangover, but also a terrible sequin pattern on my face after having passed out on an uncomfortable decorative pillow on my friend's couch. And these are only minor open bar aftermath offenses. It seems this is a lesson you have to learn for yourself, maybe even more than once. But if you haven't already experienced this yourself and you are willing to listen, please consider this a warning. Doubling (or tripling) your usual drink consumption, simply because it's free, will cost you physically the next day (or maybe two).

3   Let your shoulders drop.

It's no secret that we carry a lot of stress in our neck and shoulders. We've all got a lot going on in our personal and professional lives, and any tension is only intensified by the poor posture most of us hold as we spend our days hunched over our devices. Any time I've seen a massage therapist or physical therapist, they are always surprised at how tight my shoulder muscles are and I've had to explain that I am just a tense person—"I have a hard time letting go and relaxing." Somewhere along the way in my late twenties, I experienced the great release of having my shoulders drop. You'll know it when you feel it. It is not an ongoing change, and I haven't perfected it by any means, but I now know what it feels like when they fall, to actually relax. So I've paid close attention to what allows me to do this. The things that have worked for me are: sitting in the sun in a lounge chair on the beach by myself, or with only one other person (too many people and I'm too worried about plans or making sure everyone is provided for); getting a massage (this one feels like a no-brainer, but cannot always be afforded); morning coffee in bed with a book and no schedule; taking a bath during the middle of the day; and sitting in the backyard of my home for happy hour. If you too find it hard to relax, experiment with different leisurely activities and at different times of day and take note of which ones put your body just a little more at ease.

4   Don't defer enjoyment.

What are you saving that special bottle of wine or massage gift certificate for? I love massages; massage gift certificates are almost always on my birthday list. But when I receive them I then do this ridiculous thing where I leave them displayed on my dresser or tucked inside my underwear drawer, as if they were a motivational quote or a most valuable treasure. And I wait to use them, saying to myself, *I'll go after that weekend event on the calendar, I'm sure my back will hurt even more then.* Or *I'll wait until I've had a really stressful week and then it will feel even more rewarding.* Don't wait to treat yourself to the things that make you feel good. Go and enjoy them while you know you are healthy and that you actually can.

5   Go outside every day.

6   Do not drink well liquor at bars, it is not worth it.

Depending on where you live, it might not be called "well liquor;" this is something I learned as I moved from the south toward the north. It can also be known as "rail liquor." Regardless of what geographical area you frequent bars in, don't drink the liquor located on the bottom shelf, or off the shelf altogether. If the type of liquor is the largest word on the label or if it simply says "Vodka" across the bottle, please do not drink it. Pay the extra one to two dollars for a better drink. You'll thank me in the morning.

7 You are the only person stopping you.

In most cases, unless you still live at home with your parents, you are the only person holding you back. Not that parents necessarily hold you back, but if you live with your parents there are rules or courtesies that you should follow. As an adult, you make the rules and the plans, and unfortunately, the excuses too. Self-doubt and negative self-talk are big creators of excuses, and they can become huge obstacles that keep you from pursuing what you want. But did you notice that both of those words have "self" in them? They are also self-created. So stop getting in your own way. Take those music lessons you've been talking about for years, commit to training for a half-marathon, book a ticket for the travel plans in your mind, take actionable steps to actually stop the bad habits that you wish you didn't have. You are capable of making your wildest dreams come true, and you'll be a happier and healthier person knowing you didn't let your own mind hold you back.

8 Really good music makes people loose at the limbs.

I've loved live music my entire life. One of my favorite things to do at concerts is watch other people dance. I'm slightly reserved and not the best at letting myself go, but it brings me joy to see others do this. When you're listening to good music, you let your guard down and feel free; self-consciousness seems to evaporate. Really good music is really good at making us feel this way.

I was at a small show in Atlanta with my brother, who is also reserved and allows himself to maybe do like a slight head-bob and a foot-tap to the beat, while his arms remain crossed with his drink in one hand. I saw someone a few rows ahead of me just flailing their arms and moving their hips, completely free and feeling the music. I decided to let my body do whatever it felt like it should do, and I started dancing too. It made me laugh; it made both of us laugh. Dancing doesn't just feel good, it's contagious too. So go to a concert and then let yourself go.

9   You grow stronger only by lifting more than you think you're capable of lifting.

Every able body should try weightlifting at some point, or maybe even practice it regularly. It's an incredible act in challenging your physical body and your mental strength too. I lifted weights occasionally in high school for team sports, but never really participated in the act regularly until I had a boyfriend who was disciplined in weight training. I was a soccer player and runner who had counted on cardio and crunches and maybe did a few things here and there with a five-pound free weight and that was it for me.

What I find most interesting and challenging about strength training with weights is that you eventually have to make the jump and start lifting with a higher weight, even if you don't think you can do it. For example, I had mastered twenty pounds on each side for the bench press, but kept saying that was all I could do, that I couldn't increase the weight. You don't think you can, only because you haven't tried. Each time you lift more to become stronger, you challenge what you know you can handle in order to take on more. And you'll be surprised at what you can accomplish.

Each time you take on more, whether it be new work, a risk to move to another city, or taking on the emotional weight of a friend's troubles, you grow stronger. The real growth in our lives takes place when we take on more than we think we're capable of lifting.

10 Take note of what shuts you down.

When you allow others to shut you down, they've hit a nerve or made you acknowledge a part of yourself that is insecure or uncertain. I'm talking about situations in which an interaction with another person might make you say things to yourself like, *I can't go on, I'm not good enough, I don't have it in me.* Don't just check out or accept being shut down on this topic or task. Take note of what made you feel this way. What did they say that made you call it quits? Or what made you throw in the towel?

For me it was realizing that I let criticism about my work get all the way to the core of me, shutting me down by affecting my mind and my mental health instead of just letting it be about my work. I'm learning to compartmentalize, to not let something in one area of my life leak into all other areas of my life. So take note of what it might be for you. When is the last time you thought, *I'm going to quit* or *I can't go on,* because of something someone else said to you? You could just let this person shut you down, you could just quit. Or you could use the opportunity to identify whatever it is going on inside and improve your well-being. This interaction might have existed just to help you uncover it.

11   At the end of every day, try to recount more happiness and gratefulness than anger and discontentment.

12   An obsession with your health can become unhealthy.

Lots of people have success with diets or specific workouts. Speaking candidly, I've never really tried any diet except for that one time in college when my roommate and I attempted the Special K diet, where you only eat Special K products and then a high-protein, high-veggie dinner. It's worth noting two things: One, I cheated and ate a bunch of fruit during the day as well because I wasn't satisfied. Two, I realize as I'm writing this just how crazy of a brand play the Special K diet actually was. But the point I'm working toward is that I've never been a huge believer in diets, but I am a huge believer in discipline, and I know there is a connection there.

My mom has been an avid walker my entire life, but she has also struggled with weight fluctuations and dissatisfaction with her weight for a good portion of my life too. A few years ago, she started a particular low-carb diet and she actually had a lot of success. She was disciplined, diligent, and she saw really great results, losing twenty-two pounds in the first eight weeks. She was so excited by her results that she wanted to keep going even after she met her goal. I've seen this before with college friends who were experimenting with certain diets, who saw results and then let it go too far, resulting in being too skinny or malnourished. As counterintuitive as it sounds, it can be unhealthy to focus too much on one's weight and health. Positive results can be addictive, so be careful. Work toward your goal, achieve it, and then simply do what you need to do to maintain. Don't overdo it.

13 Confidence looks good on everyone.

How you dress your body is a way of caring for your body. The way you show up affects your attitude, which affects your interactions, which affects your outcomes. Dress your body so that you feel and therefore look confident. You should have two or three outfits for work and for play that make you feel your best. You might feel your best because the color makes you happy, or you might feel your best because the fit really flatters your body shape and makes you look strong. You might also feel your best because you were on time for the occasion, because when you have clothes you feel good about it's easier to get dressed in the morning. In every phase of my life and for each season, I've had this—a go-to work outfit, a go-to going out outfit, and even a go-to workout outfit—each of which not only looks good, but that makes me feel good about myself. Constantly pulling your shirt down or readjusting your pants leg isn't a good look. Being confidently dressed has the potential to change your entire day, but if nothing else, it can at least make you feel good.

14 Make smart food choices and make time for exercise. Or at least do one of these things.

15 Take good care of your hands. They are your most direct connection with the world.

It's often not until we are unable to use a part of our body that we realize just how important it is. Our hands do a lot of things for us; they cook and cut our food, they handle the steering wheel, they push the elevator button and turn the key, they wash our face and our hair. They hold other people's hands. Having your hand in a bandage or cast makes things difficult.

Too many times, I've taken for granted just how much we use our hands and need them. I've assumed my hands can handle it as I hurriedly opened a box I should have waited to use scissors on, ending in several deep cardboard and paper cuts across my palm. I've also assumed that I've used a wine opener so many times I could do it without looking, while distractedly talking to others, ending in a good portion of my thumb getting caught in the mix. I lost more blood than one could ever imagine losing from a thumb alone. So take good care of your hands. Wash them regularly to increase your chances of staying healthy. Trim your nails and cuticles, and don't pick them so you can stay presentable. Moisturize them; be the responsible adult who keeps hand cream on their nightstand, and most importantly, don't take them for granted. Treat your hands like the valuable instruments they are.

16 Aim to be remembered with wrinkles.

To set the record straight up front, I firmly believe in wearing sunscreen and protecting your skin from unnecessary aging—please practice safe sunning. But please also embrace the beauty of natural aging and the fact that age implies a long life and hopefully a full one too. My mom was visiting me for a girls' weekend and we were lying in bed, talking about her health, when she mentioned that she hoped I didn't remember her wrinkled face. I very quickly said to her, "Who wants to die young and be remembered with a fresh, wrinkle-free face?" I want the lines that show where I've been and what I've been through, and I want many of them. I hope her face gets even more wrinkled before I have to ever start remembering it. I hope yours does too. When the time comes, embrace physical aging; it means we've lived.

17   Test your gut to trust your gut.

The thing about having a good gut instinct and trusting it is, sometimes you need to ignore it in order to remind yourself why you should always trust it. One day I got in my car and started the engine. It felt a little weird but started anyway and I thought, *I should probably take my car in, it might not start soon.* Days later it wouldn't start at all and I had to wait for it to be towed. As I watched my car ride away with no wheels in motion, it sank in that sometimes you have to not act on your gut instinct in order to know that it's right. It's okay to test it as a way of learning to trust it.

18   Build your cave first.

I realized this while visiting a winery in Sonoma, California. On a tour, the owners took us to an underground cave they'd built to house their cellar and protect their wine. It had been built long before they ever built the winery or a tasting room on top. By building in this order, not only were they making sure they had it right before they invited others to be a part of their life, but they were also recognizing that it's much harder to break ground when there is something in the way on top of it.

Make sure your core is strong and protected before inviting others to share a life with you. I'm not referring to your abs, but rather your most inner being. Your mental health, self-confidence, and self-worth. Before you try to grow your network, take on new relationships or attempt to take care of others, make sure you are taking care of you (for me this means journaling, getting good sleep, exercising at least three times a week, spending time outdoors, and doing work that aligns with my values). Work on your cave and your character. Then work on developing new traits and attracting others to join and do life alongside you.

19 Hear the bells.

Despite what you might think, you actually know when something is wrong, off, or you need a change. Your body is often telling you, you just might not always be tuned in to it or paying attention. I went through this one particular season when I heard a lot of alarms. Real audible alarms, not ones from my body. The first one was caused by me. I was at a new job and was the last one to leave the office one night, and I accidentally set off the security alarm. The next day my car alarm went off excessively, and then my apartment complex had a fire drill in the middle of the night. It occurred to me that the world might be trying to send me a message, that something was wrong and these were all warnings for me to pay attention. It put me on higher alert the next few days, paying even closer attention than I normally do. I know this isn't always true, but I realized that in that same way sometimes our bodies and insides deliver subtle warnings or recurring sirens to get us to pay attention. Don't let these go unnoticed or keep brushing them off as a whisper. Listen for the warning bells that ring inside of you when something might be wrong or off. Listen to them, *hear* them, and act on what you think they might be directing your attention to. Maybe it's a red flag about your health that you shouldn't ignore, or a feeling in your gut that a person isn't right for you. Explore the warnings. They exist to keep you from harm and heartache.

20   Stop acting overwhelmed by things you have control over.

21   Self-preservation isn't selfish.

22   Our senses don't communicate the way we think they do.

I took a wine tasting class once and learned that wine doesn't always taste the same way it looks or smells. In the class, the other students and I were challenged to guess what a wine was going to taste like based on the way it looked or smelled. I was instructed to make note of my expectation before I tasted each glass and then record how it was correct or incorrect. My personal (and low-budget) wine drinking experience had taught me that a darker red wine would have an earthy, rich taste. But it turns out you can have a deep red wine that still tastes light, and you can have an earthy and rich-tasting white wine too. It's a good and simple reminder that things aren't always as they appear and to be open to the unexpected.

23 You cannot plan an accident.

Instead of saying, "Have fun," my dad often says, "Be careful" or "Have a safe time." To say the man is cautious is an understatement. I'm sure you often set out to "Have a safe time." But in all of his preparation and all the ways he taught me to plan ahead, to be alert and prepared, he also pointed out to me this very important learning, that you can't plan accidents and thus you will never be prepared for everything.

24 In the quiet, you'll hear things you've never noticed before.

25 Don't forget that God cares about design and the way things look.

I had this revelation while driving in my car taking in some scenery: God cares about design and the way things look. The Old Testament begins with God taking joy in and prioritizing visual design—"He created the heavens and the earth." I believe He also likes watching us enjoy His creation. Whether or not you believe in God, nature is evidence that design does matter. Don't forget to be grateful for it and to take good care of the art.

26 **If you run, you are a runner.**

When did people get so hard on themselves? I worked for a running company and had a research assignment where I would ask people if they were runners. They would respond with lines like, "Oh, I'm not a runner. I only run three times a week." Or other statements that seemingly disqualified them because of a lack of frequency, a lack of recognition, or a lack of perceived difficulty. This kind of blew my mind. Here were people who were very obviously runners, but who felt like there was a qualification or specific level of achievement required to earn the title of "runner." You don't have to do something every single day or in a certain way in order to identify with it. If you write, you are a writer. If you make art, you are an artist. If you run and put one foot in front of the other in a slightly faster motion than walking, you are a runner. Confidently identify with the things that you do. If you inwardly think and outwardly display that you are something, you will begin to believe it too.

Prompt: What is something you do that you should more confidently identify with? Not because it matters how others see you, but because it matters that you give yourself credit!

_____

_____

_____

_____

27   Never let others define your happiness, value, or self-worth.

When I started my own business, I had a former boss advise that I should set my hourly rate first and then look at competitors to see if I should modify it, but not to start out by letting another determine my value. This was good advice, as we're often quick to seek approval and validation from others in our lives. I realized how true this is for us as individuals, not just businesses. It can be so easy to become reliant on a significant other to boost our happiness, or to let the praise (or lack of it) from those around us determine our self-worth. These are things that should be defined and maintained by you. Rip out a page from this book or find a notecard and write down what makes you happiest and what you love most about yourself. Put it somewhere you can see it regularly and memorize it like you would a definition in grade school, so you can remind yourself regularly.

Prompt: When was a time you particularly valued something about yourself and what was it?

_____

_____

_____

_____

_____

Prompt: In what ways do you show yourself praise and respect?

_____

_____

_____

_____

_____

28 Perform a "Keep, Lose, Add" analysis on your life.

In my first few working years, I worked for an advertising agency that was owned by a larger holding company and changed names and ownership a few times. During one of the meetings where we were told we'd have new business cards with yet another new agency name, we were also challenged by new leadership to individually and collectively perform a "Keep, Lose, Add" analysis on our work. I had never heard of this before, but found it to be a really productive exercise, to list three things we were doing well and should keep up, three things that were bad or debilitating to our work that we should stop doing, and three things that we didn't currently do but should consider adding that would be helpful. This exercise brought greater awareness to our team's perceived strengths and weaknesses and highlighted opportunities where we could grow.

I realized how helpful this simple exercise could be for my personal life too. Who doesn't want an easily accessible list that calls out the strengths, weaknesses, and opportunities in their life? So I added it as a yearly check-in for my mental and physical health too, and I recommend you do the same. I knew there were things I needed to "lose" or stop doing, like *stop doubting every decision I make*, but putting that idea to paper made me accountable to it. Having a short list of things to "keep" doing reminded me that I was actually good at some things despite my self-doubt, and the "add" column, with items like *practice at least ten minutes of yoga every single morning* or *add strength training to my workouts*, gave me the motivation to improve or try new things. Keep going, stop, or try this instead: such simple reminders we can and should give ourselves.

Prompt: What should you keep doing, stop doing and start doing for your personal well-being?

Keep	Lose	Add
_____	_____	_____
_____	_____	_____
_____	_____	_____
_____	_____	_____

29 Explore on foot.

Whenever I visit a new city or move into a new home, I can't wait to get outside on foot, to be a little lighter and nimbler without a car or other form of transportation. Being on foot is the best and most honest way to learn the roads. Not only will it give you a new perspective, but a little fresh air is always good for the body and clarifying to the mind. You'll likely come back from a walk refreshed and empowered, because you get to decide where you'll go, how far you'll travel, and at what pace. It's one of the only things you have that much control over.

Prompt: What is something you've noticed on foot that you have never noticed otherwise?

_____

_____

_____

_____

_____

_____

30 Let nature overwhelm you.

Nature is really incredible; beaches, mountains, breaths of fresh air, these things are all really good for your physical and mental well-being. I've been fortunate to visit some beautiful places, but I also feel blessed when I'm able to see the beauty of the nature that surrounds me every day. I grew up near the beach in Florida, but the fact that I've visited the beach so many times never makes it any less beautiful. I'm grateful for the way it activates all my senses, the way I can see the horizon, hear the waves, smell the salty air, and feel the sand beneath my feet. We could easily take all of this for granted or we could be in awe of it every time. One day as I was admiring it all, it occurred to me that we won't always be able to hear the ocean, feel the breeze, and see the blue sky, so we must enjoy them, be overwhelmed by them, and be grateful for them now.

Prompt: When was the last time nature overwhelmed you? Write down the memory and what you are most grateful for about that experience.

_____

_____

_____

_____

_____

31   Your mind and body will identify your most important decisions.

I'm a big believer in pro/con lists. That shouldn't be surprising, as I'm encouraging you to write things down and get them out on paper. In addition to buying you a little time and giving you a piece of paper and a pen to fidget with as you decide, writing down the pros and cons to a situation really helps you use your rational mind to decide. It's hard to argue with something when you are staring it down on paper. Sometimes decisions come easily to me, and other times it's a full-body experience for me to reach a decision.

When I was presented with the opportunity to take a new role at my corporate job or take a big leap and start my own business, it was not just a mental process, but a serious physical one too. I had the weekend to decide and can still remember sitting with a notebook, in a full sweat, as I made more than one pro/con list. My body had let me know that this was an important and pivotal decision in my life. Not only were my thoughts racing, but my stomach was churning and I couldn't move from the couch as I labored over what each decision would mean for me and my future. If your body is engaged, in addition to your mind, it's a sign that this decision is of great meaning and importance. Recognize that, and don't make those decisions lightly.

Prompt: What signs does your body give you to tell you a decision is important?

_____

_____

_____

_____

_____

_____

_____

_____

_____

_____

_____

_____

32 You define self-care for yourself.

Self-care, as society defines it, typically includes things like yoga, massage, reading, exercise, sipping tea, and meditating. Yet I've found that sometimes treating myself to a late-afternoon snack of popcorn and a Cherry Coke feels particularly rejuvenating and restorative to me. It comforts me and reminds me of snacks I used to share with my dad after he'd get in from work when I was younger. If that does it for you, then do that. Self-care is whatever rejuvenates and refreshes you.

Prompt: What are your favorite self-care practices? Think beyond the things you've been told are "self-care" and consider what rejuvenates you the most, mentally and physically.

_____

_____

_____

_____

_____

_____

_____

33 Discover what makes you feel whole and practice it regularly.

I haven't learned or seen it all, but I've found these things to be particularly gratifying in my life: giving myself enough time (to get ready, to commute, to wind down at night), working hard, exercising, choosing friends wisely, drinking red wine, eating plenty of vegetables, brushing my teeth every day, going to sleep at a good time, smiling, and outwardly expressing gratitude for who and what I have.

Prompt: What activities in your daily life make you feel whole?

_____

_____

_____

_____

_____

_____

_____

8 PRACTICAL ADULT LIFE

If you show up at a car dealership in a taxi, you won't have a lot of leverage.

Even if you've never purchased a car or been to a car dealership, you can understand what it means to put yourself in a position to have options, and showing up at a car dealership in a taxi just isn't one of them. I had a boss who moved to Atlanta from New Jersey. His family and belongings weren't with him yet. He had been ride-sharing to work every day for the first few weeks and finally decided he needed a car. He showed up in a new car one morning and I found out that he had gone to a car dealership the night before, in a taxi. This made me laugh a little as I imagined the salespeople who eye their customers arriving on the lot and how excited they must all be to see a customer arrive in a taxi. If that doesn't look like a sure thing, then I don't know what does. If you have nothing else to leave in, you won't have a lot of opportunity for bargaining.

Adult life is a whole new level, one filled with big purchases like cars and houses, big ideas like starting a business, big risks like moving, and sometimes big repairs like leaky ceilings or a broken heart. But among all of these really big undertakings, there are also little learnings to help you everywhere. This chapter will give you some practical tips for surviving and thriving in adulthood. It will teach you what you can learn from routine daily acts and also from the leaks and the red lights you'll encounter along the way. Being a responsible adult means things like learning to be prepared, to express your expectation and to do the best you can with what you have. Sometimes that means not showing your hand, positioning you to negotiate, and sometimes that means showing up in a taxi, doing what must be done to get you to your next day.

1   Know what you need to know to survive.

I had been married for just over one year when my husband got hit in the head by the boom of a sailboat and knocked overboard, his feet dangling from the lines, which I later learned are appropriately named "lifelines." Fortunately, he was an athlete who was able to pull himself back up on the boat, making me realize that the declined sit-up exercise at the gym does serve a real purpose; it can actually save your life. And most importantly, once he was back on board, my husband was able to instruct me on what to do with the boat as he neared becoming unconscious from a serious head wound. I'd been on his family's sailboat many times, but never paid close attention, assuming that my husband would always be with me to "show me the ropes." Now I realized I should have paid better attention to the basics—I should have known what I needed to know to survive. So from that moment on, I did. Whether it's learning the ropes on a sailboat, how to stop on ice skates, or where the tab is to inflate your life vest (you think you know, but were you actually listening to or watching the flight attendant's instructions?), pay attention to the essentials that could save you or your group if necessary.

2   Take note of establishments that only have one door. It means there is only one way in and one way out.

3   Express your expectation, or don't have one.

This is one of the most important and most recurring things I've learned in adulthood, and the ways in which I've learned it might be too many to recall. Simply put, if you have an expectation, share it. Otherwise, let your expectations go. The surest way to be disappointed is to assume other people know what you want.

4   Don't take for granted that people will stop when their light is red.

My brother got into a car accident because someone brazenly went through a red light. My brother's car was totaled, but fortunately he was all right, with just some minor bruises and pain. But as I sat in the ER with him that night, emailing his bosses that he wouldn't be in the next day, I realized something incredibly important. We can never assume someone will stop when the light is red, whether the red light is a traffic signal, a law, or a verbal warning we've provided. Just because someone has been told "no" doesn't mean they won't do it anyway, so do what you can to keep yourself safe.

5   Buy a first house with plenty of projects you could do, not plenty of projects you have to do.

6 You can't freeze time, but you can freeze your eggs.

Let me start by saying I recognize the financial and physical commitment necessary for a female to participate in egg retrieval and freeze her eggs, and I realize it's not for everyone, but this is another way I learned the important lesson of putting yourself in a position to have options. I met a dear friend and former colleague for a farewell lunch one day as she was moving to the West Coast for a new job, and over lunch we covered many topics; updates on old coworkers, our new jobs, personal passions, relationships, and egg retrieval. At the time, my friend was barely into her early thirties, but she shared with me that she had just successfully "put her eggs on ice." There was nothing wrong with her health, she simply wanted to give herself options later in life. She explained that she was excited about where her career was headed and that she was in a new relationship, not knowing where it might be headed, and she didn't want to rush or put unnecessary pressure on anything, so she decided to take this part into her own hands.

At the time this option hadn't crossed my mind, but I can't say enough how proud I was of this friend for not letting her age or current relationship status affect the way she felt about her future or the possibility of becoming a mother one day. It's so easy as a single woman in your late twenties or early thirties to feel the added and very unnecessary pressure that time isn't on your side. While we can't stop time, we also can't let it make our decisions for us. Take control of situations that you have the means to, and when you can set yourself up to have options, do it.

7   **Sometimes boring is good; it can mean nothing is wrong.**

8   **Never accept "Give it a week and come back" as a mechanic's advice for how to handle your car troubles.**

In my early twenties I had a lot of car problems, including two flat tires in my first week in a new city. I continued to take my car to the very first place I'd ever gone, which had been the closest place when I had my first flat tire. Once, when I complained about the quality of work on a recent repair, the mechanic told me: "Give it a week and if it doesn't stop making that sound, come back." No way! A good mechanic is supposed to analyze and repair a vehicle, not pretend the problem doesn't exist. I insisted they find out what was wrong with my car, and then I also found a new mechanic.

9   **Always take more books than you think you need on a beach vacation.**

I once went on a weeklong beach vacation at an all-inclusive resort. My boyfriend and I each took two books on this vacation, and when all you are doing every day is rotating where you lie in the sun, you are likely going to read a lot. We each read through our books and had to trade, so my boyfriend ended up having to read (and actually enjoying) a late 2000s Gillian Flynn thriller that was definitely written for women.

The point: Pack an extra book, not like a seven-hundred-page hardback autobiography, but throw in an extra paperback, just in case you read more than you think you will. (Note that since writing this lesson, I've heard it rumored that Shonda Rhimes once didn't take enough books on vacation and that is how she discovered the Bridgerton novels. So I suppose there is a chance that good things can come from not having enough of your own material, but still pack the extra book just in case!)

10   We often like things that remind us of things we already like.

Humans are drawn to the familiar. That song you heard earlier on the radio, that healthy cereal that has a touch of cinnamon, a book you've never read with a recommendation on the front by an author you like. All of these things provide you with familiarity, and we as humans subconsciously are drawn to things we have some level of familiarity with. Remember this the next time you are sharing a new idea with a coworker or family member: pepper your pitch with the recognizable and your audience will likely be more open to or fond of your new idea.

11   There's just as much of a chance that things could get better as there is they could get worse.

12 **Always pack at least one day in advance, that way you are more likely to remember if you forgot something before you actually leave.**

13 **Don't play contact sports in the months leading up to your wedding.**

In the final four months leading up to my wedding, I could be found wearing my engagement ring on a necklace around my neck because I had broken and torn ligaments in, of all places, my left ring finger. You may have seen this lesson and immediately imagined something happened to my face (which would have also been bad), but I injured the one external body part that is actually most significant in a wedding ceremony. Seriously, what are the chances? I was playing a friendly game of football with my fiancé's extended family the Thanksgiving before my wedding the following spring. I was having an impressive game when I suddenly lost my ability to catch a pass, somehow damaging the one finger that actually mattered. My finger swelled up almost instantly, and I was grateful to have gotten my ring off before it was stuck there or had to be cut off.

In the months that followed, I saw a hand specialist for the pain and rehabilitation and wore a finger sleeve to help reduce the swelling and size of my now-very-large left ring finger. I went to get fitted for a wedding band and had to guess/hope for my future ring size. Fortunately, the month before the wedding, my finger finally returned to its previous size. I was left with a big knuckle that helps to hold my rings in place and now serves as a reminder to me to limit the potential for injuries before big life events.

14 It's okay to just do things for fun.

We've all come to let competition, profit, and ego guide our priorities and decisions for too long. Write just because you like it, not because you plan to start a column. Interview people because you want to know their stories, not because you intend to run a booming podcast. Learn to play an instrument because it relaxes you, not because you want to perform for others. Run just to explore, not to burn calories or meet a certain time. I went for a run one day without a phone or a watch. I wanted to just go for a run without any other factors or distractions, to just explore the great outdoors. It's okay to have a hobby, to be an amateur, to just do something for fun. Let go of specific goals when running, writing, reading, baking, and playing. Do it just for the act of doing it, not for the achievement or attention you might claim in return.

15 On the fence isn't a bad place to be for a little while. You can see things from there that you can't see on either side.

16 Sometimes you'll have to deal with sensitivities that were formed long before you were around.

This applies to home improvement and also to relationships. I learned this one from a leak in the ceiling of my house. After inspection, we learned that the leak was caused by the way someone had constructed the area initially and repaired it later, a reminder that we will deal with sensitivities in people and in structures that date back longer than us. Be patient and tend to them with care.

17 Make sure you can't before you say you can't.

I've said "I can't" do a lot of things. *I can't run that far* to the friend encouraging me to sign up for a half-marathon with her. *I can't be in a long-distance relationship* to myself and a guy I was dating who was moving away. *I can't actually start my own business* to all of the people who told me I should be freelancing or doing my own thing. I'm sure you've said a lot of "can't" too. I've recognized that a lot of times I say "I can't open this" about a jar of sauce or pickles, and I say that only after I've tried to open said jar on my own or with the help of some knife, opener, or other storied aid. So be sure you've tried to open it, actually attempted to run that far and ended up passing out or falling over, and tried being in a long-distance relationship that ended, or working on your own and not getting any work, before you tell someone you can't. How do you know whether you can or cannot if you have not tried?

18 Some weeks you won't feel like you have it together until Wednesday, and that's okay.

On Sunday evenings, my Instagram feed is often filled with posts from friends with the "Sunday scaries," posts from brands about the best self-care rituals for Sunday nights, and other motivational, "you can conquer this week" kinds of posts. I feel like there is a cultural expectation to have it together on Sunday evening, like that's the universal kickoff or starting line for everyone. While it might seem like this is the norm, you should know that it's okay if this isn't the case for you. Your "workweek" might very well start on a Tuesday, or you simply might not feel ready to conquer the week until it's halfway through, and both of those situations are perfectly okay.

19 As you grow, your appreciation for things that grow will also.

. . . like plants and the act of gardening. I never liked or appreciated gardening in my early twenties. Maybe it's because I just didn't have the capacity, or I didn't want to put in any extra work. Gardening is hard, and the reward is delayed. Patience is not my strong suit. But as I grew, I started to have more interest, more care, and more pride in the ability to help other things grow too. I've joked that "Millennials Excited by Perennials" should be a website or an Instagram account (maybe I'm secretly squatting on that, or maybe it's a free idea I just offered up for you), but to me it totally summarizes what it was like to be a late twentysomething in the late twenty-teens. Everywhere I looked it seemed my peers were taking on the act of nurturing and were proud to share it with everyone. First it was plants, and then even pets and children for some, but there's something innate in us that, as we age, finally recognizes our own growth and is eager to see growth in action too.

20 Don't be too frugal; good laughs and memories may await.

My mom and I went on a girls' trip to Boston, just the two of us. We don't do many extravagant things, but the last few years, we've tried to prioritize a small annual trip. I say we don't do many extravagant things, and it's true; I come from a very humble and frugal family. So frugal, in fact, that I can calculate my grocery total before I get to the checkout line because I was taught to know or pay close attention to how much each item costs. I might be overly conservative when it comes to money. On this girls' trip, my mom wanted to go on a duck boat tour, which is popular in Boston and in many other cities positioned near the water. In case you aren't familiar, a duck boat is an amphibious vehicle that operates on land and in water. The tickets were expensive, but the activity had been recommended to my mom, and she was determined we would go.

Despite my hesitancy and my stance that we did not need to spend so much money on this, we went. (Remember that lesson about being agreeable toward your parents to make your time more enjoyable; this would be a prime example.) It turned out I was wrong about the duck boat tour, it was so very fun and worth the money. I truly laughed the entire time. We had a particularly hilarious tour guide, and my mom got to drive the boat at one point. Not only was the experience itself fun, but the memories are equally sweet, and I now have these priceless photos of my mom giddy and giggling, driving the boat and afterward boasting an "I Drove the Duck" sticker. It was well worth the seemingly overpriced forty-three dollars (or something like that) per person. The thing is, we don't always get to know what awaits us on the other side of a decision or an experience, but we can't be so frugal or so cautious that we never get the chance to find out. And sure, some experiences will turn out to be lacking and indeed overpriced, but you should take the chance in case it turns out to be priceless.

21   Pack a snack.

If you know you get irritable when you are hungry, be sure to bring along some snacks for your day or make foolproof plans for your meals.

22   Throughout the year, pay attention to the items your loved ones need or wish for.

Keep a running list in a note on your phone. This way, when holidays and birthdays come around, you can surprise them with a thoughtful present they wanted but didn't have to ask for.

23   If you want more mail, send more mail.

I love receiving handwritten notes from family and friends. There is truly nothing more exciting to me than seeing personal, thoughtful snail mail in my mailbox. I realized that if I want to receive more mail, I should send more mail. In addition to birthday cards I always send, I now send notes for no reason too, and I am always excited to see a response. This taught me to put more of what I want out of the world, into the world. And it goes for more than just mail. If you want more compassion and grace, send more compassion and grace. If you want more love, send more love, and on and on it goes.

24   When you move, get new doctors right away.

When I first moved to a new city, I didn't bother with finding a doctor until I needed one, which I then discovered was a huge mistake. I was told I'd have to wait months for my "new patient" appointment. In the years and moves that have followed, I can say this almost always remains true; it takes way too long to get in for new patient appointments. So find new doctors soon after your move, before you need them. That way you are already an established patient when you do need them.

25   The host can't leave the party.

A difficulty I've encountered and a lesson I've learned the hard way is that when you are hosting a party, you can't leave whenever you want to. I have truly felt stuck as the host of a large party with guests who wouldn't leave, despite my clear change in attitude that it was time to go. It's the worst when your good time transitions into a chore of too long of a time. I love an adult dinner party or a group gathering, but I also love to sleep and go to bed early. These things have come in conflict for me before when I've been the host of a party. I was often the friend who left events at responsible times before things got sloppy, or who was known to Irish goodbye at the bar. I love having an out, so the hardest part for me is figuring out how to subtly bring an end to a good time so that everyone can have a good bedtime. You might not be as worried about your bedtime, but do keep this one in mind before you volunteer to host. And if you are worried about your bedtime, here's one trick that has worked for me. Integrate cleaning up into a subtle last call, "I'm going to put these things away, can I get you one more drink while I'm up?" And then take the time to clean up and put some dishes away while you are getting what will hopefully be your guest's last drink.

26   Figure it out while you fake it.

You've probably heard the phrase, "Fake it till you make it." It's true we are all novices at some point, with a lot to figure out along the way in work and in life. I was only three months into a new job when my immediate boss and her boss both moved on to new organizations, leaving me as the highest-ranking marketing and public relations team member at my organization, in a completely new industry. I knew a good deal about advertising and branding at that point, but my media relations and communications skills were minimal and unpracticed. I felt thrown into the fire, but I put on a confident exterior and got to work at every spare moment, educating myself and tapping into resources where I could to make sure I was doing the job and becoming an expert. I went on to fill this role full-time, receiving a promotion and a salary increase as a team was rebuilt around me. I also want you to appear confident at your job and in your daily life; I believe confidence is key. But you can't just fake it and expect to eventually make it without putting in the work. So, go on being confident and "faking it," but take the time and put in the work to figure it out, whatever "it" is, or else you'll never actually make it to the "make it" part.

27 Don't worry or complain too much about the weather.

There is truly nothing you can do about it! If it's raining for your trip of a lifetime, then you were meant to see it in the rain.

28   Important things take longer than you anticipate they will.

In my early twenties, I thought I'd land in my forever career right away, not realizing it would take time to learn what I liked and what I was truly good at. In my late twenties, I thought I'd write a book, discovering that the process would be complex and years in the making. I also embarked on renovating an old house and learned that it's safe to assume everything takes twice as long as originally estimated. There is a famous Steve Jobs quote that says, "If you look really closely, most overnight successes took a long time." This couldn't be truer; we've been conditioned to expect quick results, but that's only how it seems. Whether you are building a startup or rebuilding a home, go into it with the understanding that it might take longer than you think.

29   Always have a pencil and paper handy.

Technology has gotten the best of us. You likely don't know what to do with yourself if the Wi-Fi doesn't work or your email is down. How many times have you been found still opening up your app even when it reads, "Cannot refresh feed"? The internet went completely out at a large corporate office where I worked and truly, no one knew what to do with themselves. Everyone was pacing around or sitting at each other's desks just nervously chatting, because without technology it seemed no work could be done. I felt like we should have had some way to still make progress in our work and our day, even without our systems. Be prepared with the basics so that no matter the tech fail or snafu, you won't be stymied. Keep some printouts of what you are working on or download the files. Have a marker and a dry erase board so you and your team can brainstorm. And in the most basic way, always have a pencil and paper handy—lead is more reliable, just in case your ink pen runs out.

30 You can recognize a good cookbook by its stains and crinkled pages.

31 Just because the dispenser doesn't work, don't assume the container is empty.

Even when you're washing your hands you can be learning. If a soap dispenser isn't working, dig in, open the container, and see if there's something there. And such is the way you should live life and treat your encounters and relationships. Things may not always work right or right away; you may have to dig in and work harder to get to know someone or determine if a job is right for you. If it doesn't work on the first try, don't assume there's nothing there.

32   Everything in modification.

You've probably heard, "Everything in moderation," and maybe you even read the line above as that the first time. Well, this is a twist. There are two important things to learn here. First, modifying things for your own taste and priorities is important. I'm talking recipes, workouts, daily schedules, and jacket and pant sizes too. Don't just accept what is given to you, look out for what's best for you and adjust according to your needs. Modification leads to a tailor-made life. Second, even old sayings can be modified.

33   Always take the jacket.

I was in San Francisco for the first time, not yet aware of microclimates and unsure whether or not to bring a jacket for the day's adventure. I was afraid of being cold, but also afraid of being weighed down with the jacket if I didn't need it. A family friend suggested that I take one, and it was a good thing because I definitely needed it. Think of this lesson as a modern spin on the old adage, "Better to have it and not need it than need it and not have it." Always be as prepared as you can be for what may come.

Prompt: What is something seemingly simple you can do that will make you more confident and more prepared for your day?

_____

_____

_____

_____

_____

_____

_____

_____

34 People always say, "Things come in threes," so make sure you have a fourth good idea in your back pocket.

You've probably heard this your whole life, that good and bad things come in threes. Ideas seem to come in threes too. We've awarded the number three this all-being status as the number of balance and choice. But as everyone gets accustomed to seeing, viewing, and understanding things in threes, if you present three options, always be ready with a fourth good idea in your back pocket. It will feel unexpected.

Prompt: Practice having a good fourth idea.

Good Idea 1: _____

_____

Good Idea 2: _____

_____

Good Idea 3: _____

_____

Good Idea 4: _____

_____

35 The weakness isn't necessarily where the leak is.

Surely you've experienced a sink faucet that was broken or leaking at some point in your life. Take the time to understand why it's leaking. The cause is often not at the most obvious spot; this is true with people as well. A friend or loved one may be acting out over one issue when they're really upset about an entirely different one. Take the time to look more closely, the situation may not be as it seems.

Prompt: Is there someone or something in your life that is currently "broken"? What might the real issue be versus what it appears to be?

_____

_____

_____

_____

_____

_____

_____

36   Don't be too cool for the popular song.

My older brother and I were at a sold-out concert, Jimmy Eat World's ten-year reunion tour. Hopefully some of you in your early thirties understand just how great this was. They played "The Middle," their first number one hit, back when I was in middle school and my brother was still making CDs for me with songs he downloaded from Napster. Everyone was dancing and jumping up and down, and my brother, who has always liked whatever isn't popular, was just standing there, not singing, dancing, or moving. I reminded him of this, that you can't be too cool for the popular song; be grateful for it. It's the only reason the band is popular enough to tour in the first place.

Prompt: What are some good examples of the "popular song" in your life? Write down something you should appreciate because it made other things possible:

_____

_____

_____

_____

_____

_____

37   The greatest explorers weren't following paths.

Imagine this one yelled out dramatically from me to my dad as my family continued to wander down a trail in the mountains that we had no map for. We got lost that day, thinking we were on a simple circle trail, but we were not, and it actually felt good to be lost; it had been a long time. We live in a world of answered questions, templates, paths, and plans. We've forgotten how to be both raw and wrong, with a filter it seems we can place on almost anything. But whether it's the next time you're out in the middle of nature or you're trying to craft the perfect business plan, remind yourself that some of the world's most well-known explorers had absolutely no idea where they were going until they got there.

Prompt: Describe a time when you had no idea where you were going until you got there. What did it teach you about finding your own way?

_____

_____

_____

_____

_____

38   Give thanks.

I'm convinced things actually taste and feel better when you express gratitude for them. For me that means thanking God, for you it might mean something else. Not only does the fruit taste sweeter or the view become even more unforgettable, but by taking the time to express gratitude, you take the time to pay closer attention to the person, place, thing, or action at hand. This time of gratitude has helped to reveal many lessons for me, and I'm particularly grateful for all of the ways they've shaped my life. And especially for the opportunity to share them with you here.

Prompt: List three things you are thankful for right now.

1. _____

_____

2. _____

_____

3. _____

_____

FAREWELL LESSON

Write the book.

In the beginning, this was an action item on a list. In 2010, I wrote down ten things to do in the next ten years and "Write a book" was on that list. I didn't know what it would be then, I just hoped that someday I'd have a story to share. That same year I started writing down lessons that God was showing me through everyday events and notes I always wanted to remember about this life. Somewhere along the way it occurred to me that this content could be the book, because I knew that keeping all this insight and experience to myself was a waste. No matter what job I was at or which city I lived in, this kept coming up for me, a feeling and force inside that I must "Write the Book." It became more of a mantra than an item on a to-do list. It became something I'd write down for motivation, a reminder that this life is too short to not do the things you've always felt called to do and to contribute to this world.

If you've made it this far, I hope this book has been helpful, whether in the way I intended for it to be or in a way completely unique to you. And as we depart for now, I hope to leave you thoughtfully making plans to do that thing you've always wanted to do but haven't had the chance to yet. Whatever it may be, go write the book.

ACKNOWLEDGMENTS

I am extremely grateful to anyone who is reading this page. Thank you for reading this book in its entirety or for simply picking it up and flipping through it. If you know me and you recognized yourself in any of these lessons, a most sincere thank you for the teaching and for doing life with me. It's true that we never know when we're making a memory or a moment that will impact someone else's life; I hope you know you've made a difference in mine.

First and foremost, my biggest thank you to my husband, Ryan, my sounding board, editor, first reader, wise counsel, and emphatic cheerleader on both this book and my life. Picking you for my team was the best decision I've ever made. While the goal of a book existed before I knew you, the book we're holding in our hands would never have existed without you. Thank you for learning alongside me and for so enthusiastically supporting me and lifting me up every step of the way.

To my dearest Addie, who entered the world in the midst of me turning this passion project into a real book. You were a light, right away and always. Thank you for giving a face and a name to the person I'd been writing to all along, making this more meaningful than I ever imagined it could be. It is a gift to watch your life unfold and I am grateful every day that God chose me to be your guide.

To my mom, dad, and brother who called me "Captain Quote" growing up because of the way I'd recite famous quotations all the time. It's an honor to have you all smile or smirk as I now say, "There's a lesson in the book about . . ." I wouldn't be the person I am today without your love, nurturing, patience, and lessons in perseverance. More specifically:

. . . to Mom, thank you for telling me that I could do anything, believing that, and making me believe it too. Thank you for the big ways you support my life and my goals and for all of the little ways too. Thank you for answering the phone every time I call, whether I have a question about Addie or a question about the placement of a comma. I'm grateful that I always have you to call on, no matter what.

. . . to Dad, it's no secret that, like me, you have a lot to say. But you also have a gift for saying just the right thing at just the right time and in your own way. One of the times I said something about quitting the book process, you simply said, "You should do what will make you happy, will quitting make you happy?" Of course, the answer was no. This book is set to publish the very week you plan to retire, what a wonderful example of the circle of life. Thank you for all of your hard work, your good words, and instilling the importance of both in me.

. . . to the most recurring character in this book besides me (and for good reason), my brother, Jonathan. I wrote that it's possible that siblings are the most influential people in your life and this book is testament to that truth. Thank you for your influence, your gentle yet steady guidance, and for making everything I've ever done better, or at the very least, better looking.

To the three women who've seen me through it all and cheered me on always—Ashley, Clara, and Rachel. Thank you for being my best friends, greatest teachers, and encouragers in all that I do.

To Aunt Cotton for introducing me to the *Life's Little Instruction Book* at a very young age, which inspired me early on to recognize and record all that I learned. Thank you for all of the love you've shared and taught me over the years.

To Kathleen, Addie's Mimi, thank you for jumping in to help so I could finish this book and meet deadlines. We're so grateful for the ways you support our little family when we seemingly take on a little too much.

To Amelia, who sees what no one else does and then shares it with the world. It's such a gift to have a photo that actually captures how you hope to be known and remembered. Thank you for contributing that gift to this project and for always sharing your talents with me and our family.

To my editors:

Julia Pastore—For a first pass and the first step in taking this whole book-writing thing very seriously.

Annie Tucker—For the touchdown pass and for helping me get to the finish line, this would have been a very different book without your experienced eye. I am blessed to have had the comfort and confidence of your coaching.

To my SWP Team, Brooke and Samantha—Thank you for

making a way for female authors like me and for working with me to bring my vision to life.

To my early readers and sounding boards:

Caroline—Your persistence and perspective have been vital to me over the years and to the success of this book. Thank you for your initial read-through way back when and the encouragement that this work can make a difference.

Rachel—My sister, biggest fan, and legal counsel. Thanks for joining me on this journey in many roles and for always asking, "What's next for the book?"

Jacqueline—What a gift to have a PhD in Psychology in the family! Thank you for always asking big and good questions with me in life and particularly for reviewing those I've asked of readers in this book.

To Jacob, thanks for always being the first person to like my posts. It's a little thing that means a lot and it's just one example of how you've shown your enthusiasm for this book and my work.

To the many leaders, mentors, mentees, and clients who've opened doors for me or allowed me to hold them open for you: Leda, Jill, Jason, Angela, John, Kelly, Jeff, Ashley, Andy, Georgia, Tracey, Tracy, Rich, Lisa, Leigh, Blais, Jasmine, Adrienne, Jami, Hannah, Haley, Will, Katie, Kirby, Stacey, Jeff O, Jess, Brooke, Mike, Karima, Aisha, Natasha, Bess, and Lauren. Without each of you, my lessons in work would have been nonexistent or far less interesting.

To the inspiring and talented women who willingly and enthusiastically did an advance read of this book, thank you for sharing the precious gifts of your endorsement and your time.

Finally, thank you to the Author and Perfecter of my faith and my life. I'm so grateful to be living the story you've written for me. Thank you, God, for all of the teaching and for giving me the gifts to notice your work and share it with others.

ABOUT THE AUTHOR

© Amelia Lawrence

Michelle Douglas is a writer and mentor with a passion for helping individuals and brands uncover their reason for being and share their story. At age twenty-one she began a career in advertising and marketing, growing through work experience with advertising agencies, nonprofits, and global corporations. At the same time, she began the practice of journaling and recording life lessons, culminating in more than a decade of learnings to guide today's twentysomethings. She shares the inspiring life advice she gleaned from this practice with twentysomethings through contributor articles, online at fieldguidefortwenties.com and on Instagram at @fieldguidefortwenties. Michelle is the founder of Ladder, a brand strategy and communications company focused on social good, where she has worked with clients ranging from Olympic athletes to Harvard Business School New Venture Competition winners. A native of Jacksonville, Florida, graduate of the University of Florida, and transplant from Atlanta, Georgia, Michelle feels fortunate to call many places home. She currently lives in Annapolis, Maryland with her husband and young daughter.

SELECTED TITLES FROM SHE WRITES PRESS

She Writes Press is an independent publishing company founded to serve women writers everywhere. Visit us at www.shewritespress.com.

Just Be: A Search for Self-Love in India by Meredith Rom. $16.95, 978-1-63152-286-4. After following her intuition to fly across the world and travel alone through the crowded streets of India, twenty-two-year-old Meredith Rom learns that that true spiritual development begins when we take the leap of trusting our intuition and finding a love within.

Life's Accessories: A Memoir (And Fashion Guide) by Rachel Levy Lesser. $16.95, 978-1-63152-622-0. Rachel Levy Lesser tells the story of her life in this collection—fourteen coming-of-age essays, each one tied to a unique fashion accessory, laced with humor and introspection about a girl-turned-woman trying to figure out friendship, love, a career path, parenthood, and, most poignantly, losing her mother to cancer at a young age.

The Book of Calm: Clarity, Compassion, and Choice in a Turbulent World by Nancy G. Shapiro. $16.95, 978-1-63152-248-2. Using real-life stories, scientific concepts, and awareness tools, this timely, field-tested guide encourages readers to transform reaction into clarity, blame into compassion, and confusion into choice while navigating the turbulence of personal and professional shifts.

Think Better. Live Better. 5 Steps to Create the Life You Deserve by Francine Huss. $16.95, 978-1-938314-66-7. With the help of this guide, readers will learn to cultivate more creative thoughts, realign their mindset, and gain a new perspective on life.

Amazon Wisdom Keeper: A Psychologist's Memoir of Spiritual Awakening, Loraine Y. Van Tuyl, PhD. $16.95, 978-1-63152-316-8. Van Tuyl, a graduate psychology student and budding shamanic healer, is blindsided when she begins to experience startling visions, hear elusive drumming, and become aware of her inseverable, mystical ties to the Amazon rainforest of her native Suriname. Is she in the wrong field, or did her childhood dreams, imaginary guides, and premonitions somehow prepare her for these challenges?